Contents

Acknowledgments

I would like to thank most sincerely three of my colleagues at the
Northern Counties College of Education for their help in the earlier
stages of this book: Mr J. F. Clarke, formerly Librarian, who made
the original drawings; Mr A. Rugg, who gave me valuable advice on the
sections dealing with psychology and moral development; and Mr R.
Snowdon, who read the manuscript and advised me on grammar and
punctuation. None of them is in any way responsible for the opinions
expressed or choice of selection or emphasis.

R.L.

Introduction

Education today is so much concerned with child psychology and development that there is an urgent need for their application to games teaching in line with other subjects. To this end I have evolved sets of progressive lead-up games which start at the most basic stages and work towards practically all the well-known adult games. The aim is to ensure that children are fully involved in playing and thus gain insight into each game as a whole, while practising the relevant skills in suitable skill practices. The importance of child participation in the making of rules—and ensuing penalties for breaking them—is fundamental to each progression.

I have taken it for granted that many readers will be familiar with Laban's Principles and have made no attempt to state them again as they can now be found in a number of books, some of which are included in the bibliography.

The charts, diagrams, skill practices and rules are not intended to provide exhaustive lists, and only the briefest outlines of specific lessons are given. The reasons for this will become obvious to the reader. Circumstances vary so greatly between classes, schools and parts of the country that specimen lessons could only be misleading. In the same way, syllabuses will vary considerably from one area to another. Inevitably the teacher must decide for himself.

Headmasters and headmistresses have hardly been mentioned in this book, but they clearly have a most important influence on the attitude to games in any school. They control the money spent on equipment; they are responsible for intra- and extra-curricular activities. Their attitude to representative teams is often decisive in a junior school.

The main intention of this book is to help teachers and students in colleges of education to teach games lessons in primary schools. No attempt has been made to over-simplify the theories on which the following recommendations have been based. They seem reasonable and convincing to me but every teacher must make up his own mind. I have tried to state as clearly as possible both sides of controversial issues as I see them. I have drawn on those sources that I know best and hope readers will be interested enough to follow them up. A short bibliography will be found at the end of the book.

Throughout this book, 'he' should be understood to subsume 'she' in references to both teacher and pupil.

NOTE   In this second edition, most measurements have been metricated except in those instances where items of equipment are still normally ordered from suppliers by means of imperial measures.

1   *Games in the Context of Education and Child Development*

Class teacher or specialist?

It is generally accepted nowadays that infant teachers teach their own children all lessons whether their time-tables are integrated or not. The case in the junior school is rather different. The argument for specialist teachers of physical education is as follows:

1. Physical education including games is more specialized, more strenuous and more difficult to organize than other subjects as children grow older. The specialist teacher with his specific training, aptitudes and interest in this subject can, therefore, know more about it than the class teacher.

2. A specialist teacher can use the same organization and methods throughout a school and ensure continuity of teaching. He can be responsible for all physical education equipment in the school.

3. He is used to umpiring. He can know the best games players in the school and choose and coach the best teams to represent the school. It can be made a condition of his appointment that he will be responsible for all matches.

The case against specialization rests, in the first place, on the special relationship of the junior-school teacher with his class. The reader must, of course, make up his own mind on this point, but it will be clear in what follows that it is recommended that throughout the primary school each class teacher should teach physical education. Only he can integrate physical education activities with the rest of the children's interests in other lessons and with individual development. No specialist, that is, no outsider, can know the children as well as the class teacher. The class teacher is not teaching separate subjects but educating children. He knows each child's background, psychological and intellectual aptitudes and characteristics, and can adapt his lessons and organization to their needs. He alone can be flexible, especially in integrated time-tables or vertical streaming. Time-tables may have to be switched round without warning and lessons changed. Sometimes a class of children is so absorbed in a topic that the class teacher prefers to postpone the following period. He can adapt far better than a specialist to the many interruptions to the ordinary school day that constantly arise. Physical education lessons are not nearly as difficult to give as many people think, once the basic principles of physical activities are thoroughly understood.

The Plowden Report[1] (1967) emphasised the importance of physical education's contribution to the educational development of the child, and it is significant that the Inspectorate's survey *Primary Education in England* (1978) found that the subject received about as high a priority in the curriculum as mathematics. But with 22,228 maintained primary schools containing just over 3,900,000 full time pupils in England and Wales in January 1983, it can readily be seen that colleges and departments cannot turn out enough specialist teachers to staff so many schools.

Another argument against specialist teachers of physical education concerns the organization of physical education lessons in junior schools. Could one specialist teach all classes every day in a large school? What would happen if the specialist was very keen on football and gave less attention to the other aspects of physical education or to those games in which he had no personal interest. This criticism may also apply to non-specialist teachers, and both may attend week-end and longer courses to equip themselves better for the needs of their children. There is a tendency to think that specialist teachers are more concerned with 'teaching their subject' than 'teaching children', and individual teachers may feel this is less and less true.

Yet another argument concerns the education of the specialist. How are the colleges of education to organize his course? Is it conceivable that enough men and women students would come forward to take specialist courses in primary physical education? Would such courses not tend to be 'dead end', that is, would there be sufficient chance of promotion for such specialists later on? If the colleges integrated the primary with secondary main or wing courses, would the students learn enough about primary physical education? Men's specialist physical education courses rarely include dance. Would that not narrow down the programme in the junior schools? If the specialist was a woman, would she know as much about football and cricket as about women's games? It could be argued that the class teacher could teach dance or football as the case might be; but if the class teacher needs to teach these activities, then why not all physical education activities?

In fact, the argument for class teachers teaching their own classes is very strong:

1. The class teacher is constantly occupied in organizing group activities,

---

[1] *Children and their Primary Schools* (HMSO, 1967), par. 703

and groups for physical education lessons are no more difficult to organize than, for example, junior-school mathematics.

2. The principles of building up games, educational gymnastics and dance are similar to building up mathematical concepts. The primary-school specialist will have spent much of his college course studying child development, and should be better able to see its implications in physical activities than a specialist whose main interest may have been in physical performance at his own level.

3. The teachers in a junior school can devise a common plan for marking out playground and field as far as this is desirable, and for some system of co-operation in the use of apparatus.

4. In junior schools, inter-school matches and coaching for them should be treated as a club activity; the football, netball or cricket clubs should meet out of lesson time. They would then claim the teacher's attention no more or less than recorder or drama or chess clubs. Activities such as sailing or fell-walking would take their place in the school's extra-curricular programme at the same level as team games, and the prestige attached would be the same.

Team-teaching is a new techique involving several teachers and more than one class of children. There may be eighty children and two teachers or one full-time and two part-time teachers. Each teacher organizes the areas of work he knows best, the other teachers helping with groups or individual children. All the teachers get to know all the children and lessons can be integrated as with a single class teacher. Thus some specialization—for example, in physical education—is possible and welcome, and it avoids the disadvantages of the 'outside' specialist. Even young infants can happily learn from several adults in a team, provided they see them every day and are not worried by conflicting methods and instructions.

Laban's principles and primary school games[1]

Great changes have taken place in physical education in the United Kingdom with the introduction of Laban's Principles of Movement. These principles are well known now and their use in educational gymnastics and modern educational dance needs no further justification or explanation. The most important contribution is made by the pupils, the teacher setting the scene and wording tasks in such a way that children are able to learn by their own efforts. The variety of movements

[1]Laban, R. (1975) *Modern Educational Dance* (3rd edition). Plymouth, Macdonald and Evans.

they invent can be very large. The deeper the teacher's understanding of Laban's Principles and of his children, the greater both the variety and the quality of their movements.

In games, however, the situation is rather different. The apparatus used sets its own limitations and only limited variations or movements are useful. Moreover, as the pupils advance in skill, the varieties of movements are further curbed by the traditional forms of games the teacher needs to keep in view and lead up to. Other considerations become more important, such as co-operation with other players and decision-making. Laban's Principles are useful for analysing movements or for showing children how to vary, e.g., a throw or the bowling action in rounders. The movements can be carried out quickly or slowly, high or low (so that the ball passes the batsman at different heights) and with varying force or flow. But these variations do not make an action more or less appropriate, independent of the situations. An educational gymnastics sequence may have an inner logic which makes it satisfying to perform but this logic is irrelevant in games. A particular stroke in tennis or hockey may 'feel' wonderful but be useless in the context of the particular game. Nevertheless, the teacher who understands Laban's Principles will be a better teacher of games skills, especially in the early stages when he can set tasks which lead to experiment and invention with small apparatus. As far as nimble movements are of advantage, these too can be taught from the points of view of time, weight, space and flow. Indirectly, Laban's analysis of movement has made many teachers more observant and prepared to accept individual adaptations of standard movements according to a particular child's build and movement characteristcs. Another indirect conse-quence of the change Laban's Principles have effected in teaching methods is the fact that children are more often left to work out activities for themselves. Quite a different discipline from the imposed discipline of earlier years is now accepted and the children are given much more responsibility for their own actions. Similarly, in games, small side-team games require an inner discipline, and this is enhanced if children are encouraged to invent their own rules for their games.

Skills

In primary-school lessons, skills have to be taught, learnt and gradually applied in increasingly complex situations leading towards adult and major games. These are the questions which we should ask ourselves:

GAMES
IN THE PRIMARY SCHOOL

Second edition

R. M. LENEL, M. Ed.

Revised by Alison L. Parratt

HODDER AND STOUGHTON
LONDON SYDNEY AUCKLAND TORONTO

British Library Cataloguing in Publication Data

Lenel, R.M.
    Games in the primary school.—2nd ed.
    1. School sports—Great Britain   2. Schools
    —Exercises and recreations—Great Britain
    I. Title
    372.8'6   GV 346

ISBN 0 340 35964 1

First published 1969
Second edition 1984

Second edition copyright © 1984 R.M. Lenel
Revisions by Alison L. Parratt

Diagrams by Colonel H.M. Whitcombe

Printed and bound in Great Britain for
Hodder and Stoughton Educational,
a division of Hodder and Stoughton Ltd,
Mill Road, Dunton Green, Sevenoaks, Kent,
by Richard Clay (The Chaucer Press) Ltd, Bungay

Typeset in Times and Univers by Fleet Graphics, Enfield, Middlesex

1. Are we at present doing this in the simplest and most direct manner?
2. Are our present methods those most apt and in conformity with contemporary knowledge and research, and are we taking all the relevant factors in the child's life into consideration?
3. Should we think of a progression of skills? If so, how can we best determine this progression?

Methods of teaching and learning skills depend on what we mean by skills. We must define and classify this term. The selection of material for games lessons in the primary school should depend on the insight gained from these considerations. Selection of materials and methods of teaching should not be determined in isolation as an academic exercise, ignoring all those other factors which are relevant to children's growth and development, but each factor should be given its due weight. These factors are physical growth, intellectual, psychological, social and moral development and the social and material environment of the school and home.

Barbara Knapp in her fundamental work *Skill in Sport* uses the following definition: 'Skill is the learned ability to bring about predetermined results with maximum certainty, often with the minimum outlay of time or energy, or both.' This definition is used here in its application to primary-school games. The classification of skills, now attempted, also broadly follows Barbara Knapp:
1. Maturation skills
2. Techniques
3. Collection of actions.

1. Maturation skills are those which every child develops naturally, provided he can move at all, such as lifting his head, turning over, standing up, walking, running and hopping. All these skills are learnt in the sense that the child must practise them at the appropriate moment in his development when the muscles, joints and nerves have reached the stage when they can act together. They do not have to be taught in the sense that a technique has to be taught. Running, for example, may fall into both categories. Normal children learn to walk and run without teaching, but walking and running may later be coached as techniques in athletics. In that sense, walking and running would fall into the second or even the third category of this classification. Balance is another example. All normal children learn to balance in an upright posture but the centre of gravity changes as the child grows older. In a new-born infant, the centre of gravity is located in the lower part of the breast-bone, at five or six years of age it has moved to just below the umbilicus and at puberty it is situated just

below the crest of the hip-bone. This means that children, on admission to school, find balance very difficult and increasingly easier as their body proportions change.

2. Techniques are those actions that are technically sound and efficient and which are frequently confused with the third category. When we speak of skill practices we may mean, for example, throwing and catching techniques, or the ideal pattern of a movement; but we also frequently think of the application of these sequences of movements in a 'drill' or a very simple game, such as throwing a ball or kicking it. Books on soccer or basket-ball are full of such 'drills'. 'Beat your own record' activities are examples of games often referred to as skill practices as they are used to practise a skill. We should, however, confine ourselves in this category to the basic techniques of a movement which can be analysed as: the positioning of the body, the timing, the application of force and sequence of movements. In the teaching of this category of skills, the individual body build, stature, size and movement habits of a child must be taken into consideration as these frequently make an adjustment to the ideal sequence imperative. This adaptation of the ideal movement to that possible for an individual is also applied in modern methods of teaching swimming.

3. Skills in the third category are those that refer to a collection of actions—examples of these are trampolining or vaulting or playing football—and to those which in aggregate make the skilled games player. Barbara Knapp defines this category of skills as ' . . . an act or whole collection of actions in which there is a clearly defined goal or set of goals'. In putting-the-shot (which is an example of a technique), or trampolining (which is an example of a collection of actions), a technique must be learnt which must be technically sound and which is the most important ingredient in the skill. In soccer, however, the techniques play a relatively minor part and the adjustment of the player to the ever-changing situation is more important. The player who cannot head or kick the ball at the right moment in the game and in the right direction relative to the other players is not considered skilful, even if he can carry out the heading or kicking perfectly in a 'drill'. A player must be able to adjust to the speed and flight of the ball, the position and characteristics of the other players, the state of the ground and of the game: decision-making is all important. The ability to make decisions depends on the age, ability, intelligence and the physical and social development of the player. Decision-making can only be learnt in situations where a choice has to be made,

where the necessity to decide is obvious and where it matters to the learner. Thus, in the growing child, increasing numbers of factors can be taken into consideration but these situations must be built up extremely carefully so that children learn to make decisions gradually and are not plunged into situations beyond their comprehension. Psychological as well as moral and intellectual factors must, therefore, dictate the choice which may be presented to children so that decision-making can be developed. Where the complexity of the situation is beyond the children's comprehension, chaos results. The classic example of such an instance is that of twenty-two junior boys chasing one football. (See also pp. 15–16 and p. 18.)

Skills may be further classified, again following Barbara Knapp, into those where technique matters more than the environment and those where the environment is more important than techniques. The former skills are deemed to be 'closed' since the environment is of relatively little importance, the latter 'open' since perceptual learning and adjustment to, and interaction with, the environment (as in sailing or football) is most important. One can construct a continuum of skills from those that are most 'open' to those that are most 'closed', for example: rugby football (15-a-side), soccer or hockey (11-a-side), cricket (2 v. 11), netball (7-a-side), basket-ball (5-a-side), tennis (2 v. 2) and fencing (1 v. 1). In all these sports, both techniques and adjustment to situations and, therefore, decision-making are important; but the environment plays very different parts in rugby football and in fencing.

In rugby football the area of play is large and players are chosen to carry out different functions. Co-operation between players is complicated and very important. The whole situation changes constantly as decisions are made, and all the players must react to the changing conditions. It is essential that each player understands the total situation so that he can contribute his own techniques and carry out his special functions at the right moment. He can do so only by using his perceptor senses, especially his eyes and ears, and by basing his moves on what he perceives. Clearly memory, experience and speed of reaction, that is, decision-making, are very important—but not more important than in any other sport.

In fencing, the supple and varied use of the wrist and the strength and speed of the fencer's footwork ultimately determine a win or defeat. Yet a thorough knowledge of the rules are important, as well as keen observation and anticipation of the opponent's every move.

In both sports decision-making is vital but co-operation on the one hand, and technique on the other, play very different roles.

This classification of skills has most important bearings on the teaching of games to primary children. To the 5-year-old a ball does unexpected things and the technique of releasing the ball, letting go with the fingers, and trapping the ball, closing the fingers round it is difficult. The same is true for a beanbag or for any other small apparatus. The unexpected behaviour of the ball is a constant wonder and delight to the young child, and control and adjustment to the force and direction of a throw or kick are both difficult and interesting.

The kinaesthetic senses are slow to develop throughout childhood, and many months of constant practice are needed for specific control. The hall or playground, the other children and the teacher are often felt to be in the way and each child must gradually adjust to the environment and the group. The whole of the first and much of the second year of school life are usually needed to gain this control. The child must learn to observe the cues given him by the teacher (see Association Theory, p. 17). He must get a feel of the different apparatus such as beanbags, quoits, balls of different sizes, skipping ropes, hoops and how they may be manipulated. As control is gained, the environment can be increasingly taken into consideration. A great step forward is made when two children learn to adjust their actions to each other and the process often takes much time. The beanbag or ball must be thrown so that the other child is able to catch it or trap it, and different methods must be tried. Catching is at first an 'open' skill requiring adjustment to the cues from the eyes and perceptor senses. The time interval between observation and adjustment will gradually get shorter, but much practice and patience is required at this stage. Children must learn to face the direction of the ball or beanbag, reach out for it, and bring it in towards the body, closing the fingers round it. Many children remain clumsy because this stage has been hastened or interfered with through unsympathetic or derisive remarks or sheer lack of time for learning by trial and error, and gradual increase in control. Once the technique of catching becomes habitual it ceases to be an 'open' skill and gradually merges into those that are available for use as required. Catching has become a 'closed' skill, a technique.

In the same way, playing in pairs remains an 'open' skill until it can be done in many different situations and attention focused on the use that is made of it. The next step of playing against an opponent or intercepting in threes is such a game. As many teachers know, this is a game that is often played badly because children stand in a static line, a 'pig' in the middle having no hope of catching the ball until one of the outside players drops it. Then follows a scramble for a ball. If, however, the children can use many different kinds of throws, move in

14

the surrounding space, and dodge and jump, a much more active and enjoyable game results.

The situation changes again when two children play against two others. Each one has an opponent now and adjustment to the environment and to the other players becomes more complicated and more 'open'. The swift change from being in possession or on the defensive also requires constant adjustment. However obvious to the adult, this change-over must be learnt and understood. If an area limitation is made, the game becomes more difficult still and also more 'open' because constant adjustment to the boundaries has to be made. The next step is even more decisive when three players play together against three others: decision-making in respect of the relative position of one or the other player gains momentum. Psychological considerations make their appearance at this stage, such as the choice of groups for play, passing to a player deemed to be weaker or better than another; and these considerations require adjustment and sensitive handling by the teacher. Scoring of different kinds can be introduced, and the children may be able to make their own rules. It must never be forgotten that the process so far described takes several years and cannot be hastened beyond the children's powers of comprehension and adjustment. At the 3 v. 3 stage, targets can be introduced—but only when adjustment to the decision-making process has been accomplished. It would be better if aiming at targets as part of a game were left till the 4 v. 4 stage when the focus of attention is directed outside the group and on to the aim to be achieved in concerted action. This progression varies to some extent with games over a net but the increasing need to adjust to the outside environment remains the same. Thus each additional factor makes the skill increasingly 'open'.

In further stages, decisions as to function within a team become important and off-side rules may limit the area in which the player may play. There is a fairly rapid development in children's ability to play games from the 4 v. 4 to 6 v. 6 stage, but the many factors needing to be fully understood, the techniques, tactics, psychological considerations, area limitations, and functions within the team should not be hurried. The 'Newsom' child[1] who 'at 11 years punted footballs about eagerly enough' but 'may fail to develop skill later to participate enjoyably in team games involving large numbers of players and complex tactics' is often 'made' at this stage. He may be a slow learner or of small stature or a late maturer or simply an 'average' child; if he is not taught at his own rate at this stage he may never learn to take all the relevant factors into consideration and the gap between him and more

[1] *Half our Future* (HMSO), (1963), par. 404.

intelligent and more proficient players will increase. How many junior schoolboys have not spent a whole football lesson running forlornly behind a large bunch of boys after the ball and never kicked it even once? Eleven-a-side games are by no means impossible for junior-school children but only for the exceptionally mature and advanced pupils. The vast majority cannot cope with skills more 'open' or complex than 6- or, at the most, 7-a-side.

Theories of learning related to primary-school games

1. Conditioned Response Theory
2. Association Theory
3. Field or Gestalt Theory
4. Theories of Transfer of Training

1 *Conditioned Response Theory*

According to the Conditioned Response Theory the learner proceeds by trial and error. When good and/or effective movements have been found, the learner feels a sense of satisfaction which helps him to continue his efforts and stamp in the response that has been found to work. Bad habits are learnt in the same way as good ones and may be extremely difficult to eradicate later, as they are habitually accompanied by feelings of satisfaction. Examples of these are bad over-arm throwing by girls who have been allowed to throw from the wrist instead of using the whole arm, shoulders and hips, or a low tennis service in which the server makes insufficient use of his reach. The role of the teacher in the Conditioned Response Theory is vitally important. He must make sure that satisfaction is not felt by his pupils unless the action is as near as possible to the ideal movement the child can produce. He should, by anticipation (as far as possible), prevent the formation of bad habits. The teacher must be certain he or she is familiar with the basic requirements of a technique or game. All teachers will understand the difficulties of eradicating bad habits, since no one will change a bad habit unless convinced that a new one is better. Even then, annoyance with the old habit has to be constantly stimulated until the new habit has become established. Since so many new skills have to be learnt in the primary school, correct techniques should, as far as possible, be taught from the beginning. Another implication of the Conditioned Response Theory is that only correct techniques should be demonstrated, not bad ones, since the child may not be able to distinguish between a good or a bad technique even when it is pointed out; or he may not be able to remember the difference and will perhaps continue in a quandary, not knowing which is right.

2 Association Theory

The association between stimulus and response theory implies that habits are formed from the association of an action with a stimulus or a variety of stimuli. Thus, a particular stimulus or cue sets the particular response in motion, and good or bad habits are the result. The difference between this and the Conditioned Response Theory is that we are not here concerned with the feeling accompanying the action but with the varying stimuli which may set a particular response or set of actions in motion. Gradually the most effective responses to a variety of stimuli become habitual and the consensus of effective habits makes a good games player. The greatest objection to the Association Theory is the difference between habits and skills. Habits are very useful and are particularly desirable in the most 'closed' skills where techniques can eventually be produced without conscious effort on the part of the learner and are almost independent of the environment and thus result in economy of effort. The best examples of this are: putting-the-shot, diving or a routine in Olympic gymnastics. But habits occur whether the results are good or bad and skilled action is concerned with results. The associationists argue that progress in skill occurs when bad habits are discarded and good habits formed. The difficulty as noted in the Conditioned Response Theory is, however, the discarding of bad habits once formed. The usefulness of the Association Theory lies in its implications for 'closed' skills and in the fact that habitual responses to well-known stimuli free the mind for other considerations and are less tiring. According to this theory, games should be built up bit by bit until the whole game emerges.

3 Field or Gestalt Theory

Field Theory is fundamentally different from the other two. It postulates that the whole is greater than the sum of its parts; that insight must be gained into the whole of a situation or a skill and only when comprehension is achieved can a technique be analysed and each part considered separately. Thus, a whole country dance is taught and only when moderate success and the feel of the dance has been achieved need certain details be taken out and practised separately. The same applies to swimming strokes: movement in and

17

through the water is more important than the parts of a swimming stroke being learnt. Equally, a whole game should be learnt and practices only given for those techniques or tactics that require them, after the spirit of the game has been mastered. Insight into all the rules and the whole field of play should result in the co-operation of all the players for a common purpose. It is, therefore, imperative that games should be chosen to suit a certain stage of development of a group of children, irrespective of any age norm or the inclinations of the teacher. This theory corresponds to the development of 'open' skills discussed earlier according to which children, as they grow up, can cope with situations of increasing complexity provided always that these are not beyond their comprehension. According to this theory, insight into the true nature of a situation is continuously required, adjustment occurs as decision-making is practised and every player in a game can see his part in relation to the whole.

In Field Theory, those indications from the surroundings which help in the process of decision-making must be pointed out to children. These indications are called 'cues' and the teacher must point out cues and help children assimilate them. For example: observing the eyes and hands of a player, or anticipating the real direction of a pass or shot by a player in the process of dodging, or observing the face of an opponent's tennis racket at the moment of impact. It is not sufficient that children observe cues; they must act on them. The player with the best anticipation and fastest reaction time will be the best player, always keeping in mind that the more 'closed' the skill, the more techniques matter. Another implication of Field Theory is that not only are children required to pay attention to cues and to act on them rapidly but also to act in a variety of ways. Varied responses, adjusting constantly to the changing situation, mean that children must learn to adapt themselves and need many opportunities to do so in increasingly complex situations. This is also one of the reasons why team races are educationally useless. The situation does not vary and only one response is required in a setting of excitement. The result is a breakdown in skill (see pp. 53-4).

4 Theories of Transfer of Training

The only established fact about Transfer of Training is that it is not automatic. In modern dance and educational gymnastics, subconscious Transfer of Training has long been assumed but the evidence is against this. The reader is again referred to Barbara Knapp's scholarly discussion in her book *Skill in Sport*.

As regard the teaching of skills, three points emerge:

   a. When a difficult technique is to be learnt, the whole skill should be taught as mentioned earlier in the discussion of Association Theory. Lead-up practices may make learning more difficult, not easier. When some understanding of the basic action has been acquired, details can be tackled separately; for example, back-stopping in rounders (see p. 119).

   b. When tactical situations are important, they should be taught in their simplest form. If a major game is to be built up requiring insights into tactical situations, or appraisal of relative positions of players, then lead-up games are necessary in which the field of play and the complete situation is gradually enlarged or made more complex so that a child's growing powers of decision-making are continually challenged.

   c. In learning to learn, children are very much affected by the methods, style and organization of their class teacher. Every teacher in a primary school will understand this. On taking over a class of children from another teacher it will be obvious that they have been taught in a certain manner and have learnt to tackle problems in a certain way. Children also have their individual styles of learning, but the way a class tackles a problem is more often characteristic of the methods employed in teaching the class as a whole than the children's individual ways of learning. The teacher should be clear in his mind what he wants to achieve. For example, when tackling a 4 v. 4 game when targets are used for the first time (see p. 96), the children will, no doubt, be very enthusiastic—but co-operation between the players suddenly breaks down. They all want to shoot goals.

Now is the time for discussion of the real aims of the game so that the period of regression is short and the children, as they gain insight into the game, learn the true meaning of co-operation. As will be seen later, this stage cannot be tackled until a certain psychological readiness is reached. If this readiness is not apparent it would be better to change to a different type of game where psychological issues are not involved.

Two further points should be made about Transfer of Training. When two situations are similar, the similarities of the situation should be pointed out (as in changing from a 3 v. 3 to a 4 v. 4 game), and the transfer will be easier if it is thought out and prepared for. Thus, a short discussion might precede the introduction of the game, which will not, however, prevent the regression described above with most children. The second point concerns interference caused by the simultaneous learning of two similar skills. If the teacher, for instance, intends to organize a series of games over the net it would be wise not to let the children play, for example, padder-tennis, quoit-tennis and hand-tennis one after the other, but have some jumping events or kicking events alternately with the games over the net. This interference is not always obvious at the junior stage but since it certainly occurs at a later stage it may be inferred that it makes learning more difficult at the early stages too. Interference gets progressively less as proficiency in one game is achieved, when it will be possible to start a new or similar one. It may, therefore, be advisable not to start several similar games at the same time. Even then, differences in two similar games must be pointed out so that unconscious interference is counteracted as much as possible.

Another aspect of Transfer of Training has in essence been dealt with under *a*. It seems that Transfer of Training occurs more easily if a difficult skill is tackled before an easier one. This suggests that a whole technique should be learnt before the easier task of learning a particular sequence of movements which may be a part of it. This idea is also corroborated by the Association Theory of learning.

Physical development in the primary-school years

In the first edition of the book (1969) figures derived from the London County Council *Report on Heights and Weights of London School Pupils* of 1959 were used (then the most recent available). Later figures, derived from the work of the National Study of Health and Growth's Surveillance of Primary School Children between 1972 and 1976, are now available (see Tables 1 and 2, below).[1] Each year 8000 children from 22 areas in England (excluding the south-east) and 2500 children from 6 areas in Scotland were measured, and a questionnaire was completed by around 90% of their parents during this period. In every area all social classes were represented; in the English sample distribution according to father's occupation was very similiar to the 1971 census for England and Wales; distribution in the Scottish sample differed somewhat from this, and Scottish children were lighter and shorter than English children in all age-sex groups. (The tables refer to English children only.) A gradient of

[1]Information in this section is taken from the Department of Health and Social Security Report on Health and Social Subjects 21 (1981) *Sub-committee on Nutritional Surveillance: Second Report,* London: HMSO; and Rona, R. J. and Altman, D. G. (1977) 'National Study of Health and Growth: Standards of attained height, weight and triceps skinfold in English children 5-11 years old', *Annals of Human Biology,* 4, 501-23.

height was discernable, from south to north, children in the south of England being tallest. While most of the variation of height is due to parents' height, father's social class, number of siblings in the family and whether the father is employed or not still make a contribution to the variation of height of school children in England and Scotland.

Table 1

(a) Cross-sectional standards for height attained (boys)

Age (years)	Centiles in centimetres							S.D.
	3rd	10th	25th	50th	75th	90th	97th	
5.25	101.1	104.0	106.9	110.1	113.3	116.2	119.1	4.7
5.75	104.2	107.1	110.0	113.2	116.5	119.4	122.3	4.8
6.25	107.2	110.1	113.0	116.3	119.5	122.5	125.4	4.8
6.75	110.0	112.9	115.9	119.2	122.5	125.5	128.4	4.9
7.25	112.6	115.6	118.7	122.0	125.4	128.4	131.4	5.0
7.75	115.1	118.2	121.3	124.8	128.2	131.3	134.4	5.1
8.25	117.4	120.6	123.8	127.4	131.0	134.3	137.5	5.3
8.75	119.6	122.9	126.3	130.0	133.8	137.2	140.5	5.5
9.25	121.8	125.2	128.7	132.6	136.5	140.0	143.5	5.7
9.75	123.8	127.4	131.0	135.1	139.2	142.8	146.4	6.0
10.25	125.9	129.6	133.2	137.6	141.8	145.6	149.3	6.2
10.75	127.9	131.8	135.7	140.0	144.3	148.2	152.1	6.4
11.25	130.0	133.9	137.9	142.4	146.9	150.9	154.8	6.6

(b) Cross-sectional standards for height attained (girls)

Age (years)	Centiles in centimetres							S.D.
	3rd	10th	25th	50th	75th	90th	97th	
5.25	100.6	103.5	106.4	109.7	113.0	116.0	118.9	4.8
5.75	103.5	106.4	109.4	112.7	116.1	119.0	122.0	4.9
6.25	106.2	109.2	112.3	115.6	119.0	122.0	125.0	5.0
6.75	108.8	111.9	115.0	118.4	121.9	125.0	128.0	5.1
7.25	111.4	114.5	117.7	121.2	124.7	127.9	131.0	5.2
7.75	113.7	116.8	120.2	123.9	127.5	130.8	134.0	5.4
8.25	116.1	119.5	122.9	126.7	130.4	133.8	137.2	5.6
8.75	118.4	121.9	125.5	129.4	133.3	136.9	140.4	5.8
9.25	120.7	124.4	128.1	132.2	136.3	140.0	143.6	6.1
9.75	123.0	126.9	130.7	135.0	139.3	143.2	147.0	6.3
10.25	125.4	129.4	133.4	137.9	142.4	146.4	150.4	6.6
10.75	127.8	132.0	136.2	140.9	145.6	149.9	154.0	6.9
11.25	130.3	134.7	139.1	144.0	149.0	153.4	157.8	7.3

Table 2

(a) Cross-sectional standards for weight attained (boys)

Age (years)	Centiles in kilograms						
	3rd	10th	25th	50th	75th	90th	97th
5.5	15.5	16.6	17.8	19.4	21.2	23.1	25.2
6.5	17.0	18.3	19.7	21.4	23.4	25.5	27.8
7.5	18.7	20.1	21.5	23.5	25.9	28.3	31.2
8.5	20.3	21.7	23.5	25.8	28.7	31.7	35.3
9.5	22.1	23.8	25.7	28.5	31.9	35.9	40.6
10.5	24.0	25.9	28.3	31.5	35.7	40.4	46.1
11.35	26.1	28.3	31.1	35.0	39.9	45.2	51.8

(b) Cross-sectional standards for weight attained (girls)

Age (years)	Centiles in kilograms						
	3rd	10th	25th	50th	75th	90th	97th
5.5	15.0	16.1	17.3	18.9	20.6	22.3	24.2
6.5	16.3	17.7	19.1	21.0	23.1	25.3	27.8
7.5	18.0	19.4	21.2	23.4	26.1	29.0	32.2
8.5	19.8	21.4	23.5	26.2	29.4	33.0	37.2
9.5	21.9	23.8	26.1	29.2	33.2	37.6	42.8
10.5	23.9	26.9	28.6	32.2	36.9	41.1	48.6
11.35	26.1	28.5	31.4	35.7	41.1	47.3	55.1

NOTE: these tables are reproduced by kind permission of Dr R J Rona and Dr D G Altman.

A comparison of the median (50th centile) heights and weights of children at 5 + and 11 + years shows the very considerable differences in heights and weights of children on entering and leaving the primary school. Boys are likely to grow some 32 centimetres and girls some 34 centimetres; corresponding increases in weight are over 15 kilograms for boys and more than 16 kilograms for girls. Even more startling are the differences between children in the same age group. Compare height at the 3rd and 97th centiles (Table 1) at 5.25 years: the variation can be as much as 18 centimetres for both boys and girls (standard deviation 4.7 and 4.8 centimetres respectively). At 11.25 years, it can be 24 centimetres for boys and 27 centimetres for girls (standard deviation 6.6 and 7.3

centimetres respectively). Similarly with weight (Table 2): the variation at the 3rd and 97th centiles at 5.5 years can be nearly 10 kilograms for boys and 9 kilograms for girls; at 11.35 it is over 25 kilograms for boys and 29 kilograms for girls.

The figures for the National Study of Health and Growth are very similar to the heights and weights recorded in the 1959 study of London children of primary school age. Girls are still shown to be slightly heavier at 11 + and the tallest girls are taller than the tallest boys, probably because the growth spurt has already started for them.

The figures immediately come to life if one looks at a class of children and realizes the very large differences just mentioned, that is, of height and weight. These differences are bound to influence the preparation of games lessons since there are such striking variations in normal children. Such physical differences can be explained by considering the following factors:

1 *Heredity*

Children differ not only in height and weight but in stature, body-build, shape and, most important, in velocity of growth according to the genes which they have inherited. Some children mature earlier and some later than the mean, and those children who differ markedly from the average are called early or late maturers respectively. Early maturing children are ahead of their contemporaries right through childhood and late maturing children are correspondingly retarded, the effect being cumulative. In any one primary-school class, differing heights and weights may be explained either because a child is naturally large or small in stature, or because he is an early or a late maturer. The effect of early or late maturing can be seen in general development, and the class teacher will be well aware of it.

2 *Sex differences*

Differences between boys and girls occur at birth. Skeletal development shows girls to be 4 weeks ahead of boys on average and this difference in skeletal maturity is maintained until puberty which girls reach, on average, 2 years ahead of boys. The effect of skeletal difference is, therefore, cumulative, but the boys' adolescence spurt is much larger than the girls' and their final height, weight, heart diameter and strength is about 10 per cent greater than girls' on reaching maturity. At primary school, however, there is little difference in strength between boys and girls. Another difference between boys and girls from birth is the boys' longer and thicker forearm

23

relative to upper arm, legs and other parts of the body. Boys' grip in both hands is a little stronger than girls' and increasingly so after puberty. There is no sex difference in arm thrust and little in pull before puberty. The longer forearm gives a boy better leverage, especially at the elbow joint and this probably explains the boys' better scores in throwing a ball.

Growth gradients in arms and legs also show differences between the sexes. Girls' arms and legs reach adult level earlier than boys in conformity with their generally earlier maturity. A more important point about the organization of growth in the limbs is the fact that hands and feet grow towards adult size before calf length and forearm length, and these in turn before upper arm and thigh. Feet and hands grow towards maturity at about the same rate during the primary-school years but the upper limbs are a little ahead of the lower ones. This shows clearly in infants who can manipulate many objects successfully with their hands before they can use their feet with similar dexterity.

3 The secular trend towards earlier maturity

This trend, common to the whole Western world, is beginning to affect the junior school in particular ways. For more than 100 years children have reached maturity successively 4 months earlier each decade. In 1860, the mean age of girls reaching menarche was 16 years and 7 months, in 1976 it was 13.1 years with a normal spread from 10 years to 16 years.[1] It is not clear whether this trend is continuing or not, but even if it is not, the earliest maturing girls are even now reaching menarche in the junior school. The first signs of puberty precede this important stage and the greatest height spurt is nearly always completed before menarche. Early maturing girls are, therefore, growing very fast from about 9 years onwards and this is independent of stature, although more large girls than smaller ones reach maturity early.

In boys, the breaking of the voice may be considered a similar climax in adolescence, but it rarely occurs in the junior school since boys on average reach puberty 2 years later than girls.[2]

Another feature of the secular trend is the rising height of the adult population. In the 5 to 7 age group, children gained about 1 centimetre

[1]J.M. Tanner: *Education and Physical Growth,* 2nd edition (Hodder and Stoughton, 1978), p. 32.
[2]Tanner: *Education and Physical Growth,* p. 40.

and 0.5 kilogram per decade between 1880 and 1950 and these figures increase to 2 centimetres and 2 kilograms during adolescence. Final height increased by about 1 centimetre per decade.[1] Clearly, this increase in height and weight continues in the 5 to 7 age group right through the 7 to 11 age group and beyond. In terms of primary-school games, this means that children need more space, for example, for throwing; and they can run faster earlier. But whether earlier skill learning has other implications is debatable since so many factors contribute to this.

4 Physical differences between adults and primary-school children

Body proportions

Children grow taller with great regularity after about 4 years of age. As the limbs grow longer, balance and leverage become easier, the centre of gravity drops a little and the child is much steadier on his feet. Off-balance positions can be speedily corrected and boys rarely mind a tumble. The length of the trunk increases very much at puberty and the limbs do not stop growing until full skeletal development is reached which usually occurs about 2 years after menarche or change of voice. This period is, therefore, unlikely to occur in the primary school and precludes anything like adult strength and leverage.

Muscular development

There is also much less muscular development before the adolescence spurt than during and after it, but growth is steady during the period of 5 to 11 years. The large differences between children sometimes mask the real increase in strength in the smaller children. It must be remembered that individual velocities of growth affect all children variously. In relation to adults, children are much less strong and have less endurance, but opportunity for exercise can make a great deal of difference. It would be interesting to see experiments conducted into the effect on primary-school children of living in high blocks of flats which must surely restrict their movement opportunities. Professor J. M. Tanner thinks that lack of exercise has little effect on physical growth: 'there is little to suggest that muscular exercise in children would cause a lasting muscular enlargement'.[2] But it may well have considerable effect on skill.

[1] Tanner: *Education and Physical Growth*, p. 115.
[2] Tanner: *Education and Physical Growth*, p. 110.

Pulse rate and metabolism

Pulse rate and metabolism are faster in young children than in adults. Exercise increases the circulation of the blood and, since this is faster, the younger the children the quicker they get warm on a cold day. The teacher, not the children, needs extra protection against cold, especially since the teacher gets much less exercise than the children in his class. This does not mean that the teacher should be encased in clothes that make him practically immobile, but he requires sufficient warmth to enable him to give full attention to his teaching.

Intellectual development

1 *Concept formation*

Piaget's conceptual scheme of child development based on a close study of children has stimulated a great deal of experiment and received considerable support. He postulates that concepts arise out of the child's earliest experiences. Sense impressions form organizations in the brain called schemata to which new experiences are assimilated and through which schemata are modified; this modification is called 'accommodation' and occurs in well-defined stages. The stage from 4 to 7 years is known as the stage of 'Intuitive Thought'. Gradually, during this period, thought increasingly precedes action; the child can visualize what he is going to do before he carries out the action and indeed, he could do this in the preceeding stages but at a simpler level. This process, called 'Internalization', is now more complex, but the child is still only able to grasp one relation at any one time. Moreover, he cannot, as yet, reverse the process of thought in his mind and return to his starting point. A sequence of events, for example, moving from one group place to another, must, once established, always be carried out in the same order; a ball is always thrown in one direction; children move round the playground in one way; they climb up at one end and come down at the other of a set of educational gymnastics apparatus. It is virtually impossible at this stage to break such a habit, once established. The teacher must anticipate the forming of such habits if he considers it undesirable; for example, a ball can be thrown or used in many different ways, children can move about in many different directions, educational gymnastics apparatus can be approached in a variety of ways. What the children cannot do at this stage, at least at first, is to think of two points at once or go back to a starting point in reverse order.

Piaget calls his next stage in the development of thought, normally covering 7 to 11 years, the stage of 'Concrete Operations'. Children are still, in thought, bound to objects and cannot as yet manipulate a series of alternative hypotheses. They are gradually able to reverse their actions in their minds and take more than one factor into consideration. In games, children learn to play with more than one other child, choosing appropriate movements, speed, directions, and they can make decisions about relative merits of position and character of other players. This stage, as mentioned earlier, widens the child's ability in playing games and is the first step towards playing games in an adult way. It is not reached by all children at the same time; the teacher should know the children's development in other subjects and not demand strict adherence to rules before they can be fully understood by the children. This does not mean that rules should not be made, but comprehension and the ability to take more than one factor into consideration are prerequisites of more than mechanical obedience.

The child is now ready to begin preparatory games, which are often called 'lead-up games' (the term used in this book). The rapid change-over from attacking to defending play is now possible—and not before; targets can be set up and the direction of play can be reversed rapidly. Even so, children often get confused as to the goal they are attacking and at first need clear instructions and reminders.

The stage of 'Formal Operations' follows the stage of 'Concrete Operations'. Many variables, many ideas can be thought of in turn and hypotheses constructed. This is the age when children turn to tactics and think them out before a game starts. For instance, they can consider the various positions of the players, their reputation, the state of the ground and of wind and weather. They can change rapidly from one sequence of moves to another and adapt to the fortunes of the game. It must not be thought older juniors are never capable of 'Formal Operations'; but the majority are not, and, like the process of 'Reversibility', the advance to this stage varies greatly from one child to another. It is quite useless to attempt to teach children beyond their mental age and it is a crime not to teach up to it.

2 The spread of intelligence in different age groups

For all practical purposes the teacher will find it useful to think of intelligence as being whatever is described by the results of intelligence testing. This is the sense in which the term Intelligence Quotient is used here. F. W. Land, Professor of Education at the University of

Hull, said in a lecture at the Institute of Education in May 1961 that at the age of 5 the normal spread of I.Q. is 3 years; so that, on admission to school, children may have a mental age of only $3\frac{1}{2}$ years or as much as $6\frac{1}{2}$; at 10 years the spread has widened to 6 years, some children still having the mental age of an average 7-year-old but others of 13-year-olds. At 15 years the corresponding figures are a spread of 9 years, some children having a mental age of $10\frac{1}{2}$-year-olds and other of $19\frac{1}{2}$-years-olds. About two-thirds of an age group will have an average mental age with an I.Q. of between 85 and 115, that is, either just below or above the norm for their age groups. The other one-third are equally divided into those with a higher or lower I.Q. Only 17 per cent of any age group will, therefore, be really advanced and, in terms of games, not all of these will be interested in competitive games. All the same, it will be probable that the players in a junior-school team will be amongst this 17 per cent, although some children of greater maturity, stature or strength but lower I.Q. may also find a place in it. I.Q. tests are normally used as group predictors and do not take experience into consideration or the fact that interest can overcome mental limitations. It would be interesting to investigate some junior-school teams with these factors in mind. The question whether or not junior schools should or should not have representative teams is a much wider one. Here it can only be discussed in relation to intelligence and only as to whether or not children in their last year in the junior school are intellectually able to play with the necessary comprehension of tactics. The answer from this point of view must be that some children very likely are.

At the other end of the scale there are the children with a low I.Q. Contrary to the popular view, children with a low I.Q. tackle all subjects including physical education in an unintelligent way. Furthermore, they are often clumsy or unable to accomplish complicated co-ordinations or cope with sequences of events or fit into intricate joint operations, especially if the situation demands swift adaptation and changes of plan.

The question of grouping in games in streamed and unstreamed classes can now be introduced. Very likely, ability groups in games will be forced on the teacher so as to do justice to the most and least intelligent.

3 *Intelligence and physical growth*

Professor J. M. Tanner in *Education and Physical Growth* discusses two other factors in relation to intelligence which are of interest here:

a. The more intelligent children, according to intelligence tests, tend to be the physically larger children who are on average mentally more advanced also. One must not confuse large size with early maturing, but there seems to be a definite correlation between these.

b. There seems to be a further correlation between body size, socio-economic group and intelligence. Modern evidence suggests that in adults 'there is a quite definite increase in body size from low to high socio-economic groups; and there is also a definite increase in I.Q.'[1] (though it is likely that an environmental factor is involved). Moreover, the larger the family, the progressively smaller and later maturing and also the less intelligent the children.

These points must not be taken indiscriminately. Not all large children are intelligent, not all early maturing children are intelligent, and the younger children are not all smaller and less intelligent than the older children in the same family. But the evidence as reported in many studies, including one by J.W.B. Douglas in 1960 for the Department of Public Health and Social Medicine, The Usher Institute of the University of Edinburgh, seems conclusive. In relation to primary-school games, both factors indicate further the large differences in physical and intellectual development, especially in older primary-school children. It follows that in non-streamed and family groupings, games at varying intellectual levels need to be played, but even in streamed classes the differences in stature and maturity make this desirable.

Other psychological considerations

1 *Individual play*

A young child's world is necessarily small. He can neither observe nor comprehend too complicated an environment or situation. Within their own horizon children are often capable of a subtlety surprising to an adult. But their world is circumscribed. Both opportunity to experience relationships and see and use things widen a child's mind. Generally speaking, the more varied the total environment the better, but if the demands of the environment become too complicated, young children cease to take any notice; if the demands have too great an element of stress in them, children break down just like adults.

[1]Tanner: *Education and Physical Growth*, pp. 44-5.

In infant-school games there should, at first, be many different pieces of apparatus available for free play. No demands about learning should be made at all. When children are ready they will ask the teacher how to use a piece of apparatus properly, but even before this the teacher will have moved about amongst the children giving many helpful hints. Nowadays, one sees little fighting amongst 5-year-olds but outbursts of temper still occur; the teacher can anticipate much friction by laying down rules about apparatus, and making sure each child has his own piece. If a favourite type of apparatus is in short supply, then it has to be used fairly in turn.

The first skills to be learnt correctly, such as catching a beanbag, will be improved by 'Beat your own record' activities. A child is concerned with his own achievement. If he is asked to count aloud (for example, how many times he can throw and catch a beanbag), this sometimes sounds like a chant—far removed from the activity. The relationship between the action and the counting has not yet been established. When a child is asked how many times he caught his beanbag he will say any number that comes to his mind; if the teacher is foolish enough to ask another child and he mentions a bigger number, the following children will all have scores at least as high as the biggest one mentioned. Children at 5 years old seldom think consciously of cheating but they all want to be best and first and cannot admit another child to be better than themselves. The following stage, when they begin the slow process of adapting to this painful fact, is often accompanied by tears and quarrelling. It may take a consider-able time, as much as 2 or 3 years, for children to look on other children's skill and achievement objectively. Not until children can do this to some extent can any small-side team game be fairly played. Rules even then must be quite simple and straightforward and avoid arguments as much as possible.

2 Extended groups

The extension of groups and rules should be co-ordinated with the aquisition of skills. If skill exceeds the ability to co-operate, many different skills can be played—each at a comparable intellectual and psychological level. If co-operation exceeds skill, many very easy games can be played, the children making their own rules. The teacher may be astonished by the subtlety of the rules children impose upon themselves but will be well-advised not to let this process get too complicated. The teacher must not expect the same rules to be remembered the following week but should allow for the changing ideas of children of primary-school age.

As shown in the discussion on 'open' and 'closed skills (pp. 13–16), the number of players can gradually be enlarged. How should the groups be chosen? It will be realised that, in some local education authorities, classes are today organized in family groups or vertical streaming and this may present some difficulties. The teacher should look on this realistically. In the classroom the younger child will feel the protective presence of older children and will at one time be drawn into a common activity, whilst at other times he will work at his own level. Why should this situation be handled differently in the games lesson? Certainly at first there should be no compulsion to learn. If the class is too big for effective individual teaching, the teacher can collect groups of children of similar ability for demonstrations of skills. No doubt the younger children will sometimes listen to the coaching of the older ones and perhaps try the new skill. If children are asked to show their solution to a task there is no harm in the youngest children stopping what they are doing and watching; but mostly they will be too occupied with their own games.

The change-over from playing individually to playing in pairs occurs at widely different times. Many 6-year-olds enjoy it, but some 7-year-olds are hardly ready for it and 5-year-olds but rarely. In any case, individual work should be carried on long enough so that children are thoroughly familiar with and can handle confidently a variety of small pieces of apparatus in many different ways. This width of experience and skill is often regrettably neglected, even with the most familiar pieces of apparatus.

3 *Choice of partners and groups*

But how should partners be chosen? In a small class the children may know each other well and choose partners predictably and quickly. They will change their best friend frequently but have no difficulty in choosing a partner in any one lesson. In very large classes it may be quicker to say 'Stand next to the child nearest to you', and look out for the two or three terrors amongst the children whose lack of stability can wreck a most carefully prepared lesson. They must be separated and given more stable children as partners. The same stable children must not be chosen too often unless some feeling of friendship becomes established. On the other hand, it is bad for an already unstable child to have a different partner every lesson. The dilemma can only be pointed out and not solved. Each teacher must act according to circumstances and his own inclinations.

With older children, friendship groups are generally best but there are many provisos. Once more, difficult children must be placed so as not to disturb other children's games, while not being singled out to make them conspicuous. Sometimes friendship groups cut across intellectual and skill levels. If only one or two slow children play in a more advanced game they may be 'carried' by their friends. Junior children can be both cruel and tolerant if they feel a child is too difficult, clumsy or inexperienced. It may be better to move such a child to an easier situation. If, on the other hand, a clever child is playing in a generally slower group, giving him special jobs to do (like keeping the score) may keep him sufficiently occupied. Family groupings may be helpful as children are used to differences in age, size and ability.

4 Leadership

This is a most important subject in group formation. Natural leaders arise at all levels of ability. This is as true of educationally sub-normal children as of the most gifted, and at all ages—even at kindergarten level. The ability to lead other people is a most valuable asset and needs to be given full scope. In the primary school, children are usually delighted to be chosen or asked to volunteer for special jobs, and they take them on willingly. The teacher must be sure to bring out and not stifle any aspirations and deal tactfully with the over-ambitious children.

One of the best ways of using such powers of leadership is letting children referee for each other. Supposing four games of 6-a-side are being played (or six games of 4-a-side), three (five) umpires are needed while the teacher is coaching the other game. Alternatively, the teacher can let each team vote for a captain, the captains keeping the score and making decisions about fouls; when they fail to agree the teacher is the final arbiter. The teacher can appoint team captains, but this curtails both the choice and the responsibility of the team members. Sometimes suitable children, especially girls, feel shy in taking on such leadership. They should never be forced. There are plenty of jobs such as responsibility for equipment which they may willingly take on, until—perhaps gradually—they feel more able to cope with jobs involving other children.

5 Umpiring

Umpiring or decision-making in one's own or other people's games can be started much earlier than most teachers think. The teacher cannot possibly be with each game at the same time and is, therefore, obliged to delegate responsibility. He should stand in a position where he can observe the whole class, but he cannot hope to coach effectively more than one game at a time. A few minutes with a small group is more effective than 30 minutes with the whole class. At the same time as the games get more complicated and more rules are needed, children also learn to take more responsibility. Some handicapped children make excellent umpires. They enjoy being part of the game though not able to join in. For example, a child may have an arm in a sling, but the other hand could well manipulate a whistle.

6 *Motivation*

This rarely poses a problem in the primary school although some children are lazy or frightened or suffer from lack of sleep. The better the teacher knows the children, the better he can deal with these problems. As in the case of unstable children, there is no easy solution and each case must be dealt with on its merits. If a child hates a certain type of game, a variety of games may be feasible. Sometimes children find difficulty with spectacles or hearing aids, but these can often be fixed firmly round the back of the head. The teacher can get expert advice or use his ingenuity. Bullying by larger children must be firmly dealt with the very first time a teacher notices it. He must follow up any such discovery during playground duty and possibly in talks with the children, the headmaster and the parents, and see that children are not bullied or do not bully others on the way to and from school.

Far and away the best motivation for primary-school children is their trust in the fairness of the teacher and his ability to make his lessons interesting. Primary-school children can, without difficulty, be fired into taking an interest in so many activities. The only boring thing for them is to play the same old game week after week.

Socio-economic considerations

Students in colleges of education are often hard to convince that socio-economic considerations affect games teaching; more rarely they over-rate them. It depends on their own background and experience.

1 *Rules*

The social background of a child often shows in his attitude to other children and to the rules of the game. Those from poor backgrounds are more frequently casual in conforming to rules, whereas those from middle-class homes have often greater pressure put upon them to conform at home. The result in games is that in middle-class areas rules are more readily accepted and children often co-operate earlier than in other schools. Apparatus is also collected and put away more rapidly where social pressure at home has taught a child to look after his own things and take responsibility for them.

2 Dress and equipment

In middle-class areas a school fund often provides more equipment than the L.E.A. may be able to allocate or the headmaster buy. Special clothing is more easily obtained and children rarely go without plimsolls and games shorts, and blouses and shirts. In less fortunate neighbourhoods, the teacher may have a great struggle to obtain suitable equipment and clothing, and they are frequently used more carelessly or lost and have to be replaced more often.

Children sometimes object to changing for games lessons. The teacher should be firm about this. At the very least, footwear should be changed and sweaters removed. At best, special shorts and T-shirts or blouses should be worn by girls and boys. For older juniors a system of changing, such as boys in the cloakroom and girls in the classroom, can be adopted. Infants should be trained to help each other. It is possible for a row of 6-year-olds to stand one behind another, each buttoning up the back of the dress of the child in front. A school helper can be very useful in dressing and undressing the youngest children and in the summer the teacher should not hesitate to have his class in pants (and vests) out-of-doors. In cold weather a sweater should be worn until a child is warm but discarded as soon as possible. Some children are lazy about dressing or have not been taught to cope with shoes and ties. The teacher must consider time spent on training children to cope with their clothing as time well spent.

Coloured braids are a very useful and cheap item for children to wear, as they serve as a quick means of team identification by teacher and children alike. Bibs, traditionally used in secondary schools, can be equally effective for juniors if they are numbered rather than lettered. They have the advantage of being easier to see than braids.

Some children constantly bring notes from their parents asking the teacher not to let them change or even to excuse them from the lesson.

This is rarely necessary. If it is, then the child would probably be better off at home. If children get hot in a games lesson and then cool off in the classroom, they should have a sweater or jacket to put on. A talk between the headmaster and the parents can sometimes put this right, but some over-anxious parents are more difficult to educate than their children. The teacher must avoid conflict with the children's homes while keeping up his own standards.

Bib

Moral education through games

A good deal has been written about the value of games in forming character. There is no doubt that in the United Kingdom games are played with a view to fairness rather than to winning, and that to be a good loser is held to be as important as a modest and graceful victor. These sentiments are conveyed as much by the general culture as by specific teaching. They are not, as shown in the discussion of psychological problems, natural to young children.

Piaget postulates the following stages in the development of the moral judgement of the child[1] and he separates the development of the use of rules from the understanding of rules.

1 *The development of the use of rules*
a Motor-individual Stage

At the earliest stage, play is purely individual but children visualize their play. For example, they put marbles in a pyramid or in a series, or they arrange their toy cars in a special way.

b The Egocentric Stage

Between the ages of 2 and 5 and until he is 7 or 8, the child notices

[1] J. Piaget: *The Moral Judgment of the Child* (Routledge, 1932).

rules which adults have made and imitates them without at all understanding them. He plays by himself or side by side with other children but without bothering about them and without trying to win. He imitates older children but uses examples or rules in a purely individual way, hence the term 'Egocentric Stage''

c The Incipient Co-operation Stage

This stage lasts from 7 or 8 until 11 or 12 years. Each player now tries to win and all the children in a game may come to an agreement about the rules of the moment. They are not concerned with universal rules and, therefore, rules even for traditional games vary from game to game and may be mutually exclusive on different occasions. For example, in some skipping games all the children must run right through the rope but in others they must skip in the rope for so many turns.

d The Codification of Rules Stage

At about the age of 11 or 12, all the members of a group know the same rules and use the same procedure. A code or rules is therefore to be observed.

2 *The development of the understanding of rules*

a. From about 2 to 7 years of age the rules are not yet binding, either because they are purely motor or unconsciously received. For example, the child knows a game always starts in a certain way but where this start takes place or even the form of it is not yet understood. This first stage continues until nearly the end of the Egocentric Stage.

b. The second stage may overlap the previous one to some extent. Piaget suggests that it lasts from the age of about 6 to about 10 years. Thus is overlaps the end of the Egocentric Stage to the first half of the Co-operation Stage. Rules are now regarded as sacred and untouchable, made by adults or older children, and thought of as lasting for ever. Every suggested alteration strikes the child as a transgression. Students on teaching practice find it very difficult, for example, to change the children's rules about getting out apparatus and putting it away, or giving out art and craft material. This may be compared with the paragraph on habit formation (see Association Theory, p. 17).

c. When a child is about 10 or 11 years old, he sees a rule as a law due to mutual consent which must be respected by each individual player who wished to be regarded as a loyal member of a team; but rules may now be altered if all the players agree.

There has been some controversy over the beginning of each stage, but, as with Concept Formation, the order of succession is not in doubt. The child's ability to see beyond his own personal needs and ambitions grows slowly and sometimes painfully. Here again, the case for introducing gradually more complex situations in which unselfishness is not only approved but seen to be useful and even necessary is very strong. How else can young children comprehend the greater glory of their team winning and their own part in making this possible through co-operation with their fellow team members? The appreciation of each other's capacities and special skills is very important, only equalled by the teacher's need to realize that some junior children just do not like team games. It sometimes comes as a shock to children, as also to their elders, to discover in a seemingly incapable team member an excellent performer at ice-skating or horse-riding or swimming.

To the teacher, the idea that the proven leader or fair games player can also be quarrelsome and difficult in other contexts should not come as a surprise. Therefore, too much should not be made of any one side of a child's character. What is thought to be right or wrong is not accepted equally by all members of society. There are large class differences. The teacher must guard against unsuitable treatment of children who have been brought up differently from himself and especially those who unconsciously make different assumptions. It is impossible to prevent conflicts arising in games lessons. Learning role-playing for example, behaving differently with different sets of people, is a necessary accomplishment for all children. Where the roles a child plays at home and at school most nearly coincide, least conflict arises; but the teacher must face the fact that for some children the new role demanded by the school may be in conflict with the moral standards of the home. The new role at school may be a necessary one for a child to learn and the teacher must not abdicate his role as leader and guide. Games at all levels give good opportunities for moral guidance, but the necessity and good sense of every demand made to children to whom these are not obvious must always be emphasized.

All children need to learn not to give secrets away, to be loyal team members and fearless leaders, to be unselfish, considerate and courageous. Every teacher in every games lesson will come up against moral issues, and his own behaviour and example will be of more importance to the children then either admonition or punishment.

The teacher and the class

The teacher must be concious of his own role in relation to the children. He is bound to be physically larger, and both intellectually and morally will think in different terms from primary-school children. But he must understand how primary-school children think, and in his dealings with individual children he is constantly on view. He must try neither to favour nor dislike some children and this is surely the most difficult task a teacher has to face. He cannot act as leader and guide unless the children trust him and he must never abuse their trust. His own exemplary standards are of the utmost importance in games. Why should children play according to rules if, as soon as the teacher arrives, he can break them with impunity? Why should the children change their clothes if the teacher does not? The closer the relationship between teacher and pupils, the more such questions matter.

The teacher must prepare his games lessons. If he takes the points previously made into consideration, he will appraise the children's needs and organize the lessons accordingly. More complicated organization and preparation is necessary the older the children get. Pitches need to be prepared before the lesson can begin and co-operation with other teachers can avoid much duplication of effort. Equipment must also be ready. The tidier all members of staff are, the less equipment will be lost, thus avoiding frustration in subsequent lessons.

The children should understand the organization of equipment and which part of a playground or field they are to use. They need to follow a plan which, if adhered to, can save much time and confusion. Here the teacher may make a difference in his mind between training and education. He must train the children to return all apparatus to appointed places, to stop moving if he blows his whistle or calls 'Stop'. He must train the children to change quickly and help each other quickly. But he will educate them by teaching new skills and games.

There is a great temptation for the teacher to avoid complicated arrangements of pitches for group games. How much easier it is to use eleven braids and one ball! Undoubtedly the larger the class the harder it is to resist this temptation. But to be fair to the children, nothing less than careful organization will do. To 'stretch' each child to his utmost ability is a fundamental educational principle which applies just as much to games as to any other kind of lesson.

Teaching the child insight is complicated. A series of charts on the wall will help to show older juniors the lay-out of pitches, the starting positions of players and the principal rules. Where rules and scoring are to be invented by the children, this can be clearly shown. Charts, diagrams and rules must be discussed by the children and teacher, otherwise no insight is gained and the effort of producing the charts is wasted. Sometimes it is better for this discussion to precede the first lesson in a new unit of work, sometimes after the first lesson, and subsequently whenever the teacher feels it is helpful.

Syllabus and lesson planning

The better the teacher knows the children, the better he will be able to prepare both a syllabus and units of lessons. If a teacher does not know the class he will only be able to prepare a syllabus in the broadest terms. He can, for example, propose to start the school year with throwing and catching games, followed by a unit of hockey, shinty or football games. In the late spring it may be possible to have a unit on quoit-tennis and running practices for sports days. In the summer term volley-ball, rounders and cricket games can be played with two weeks of practices for the school sports. But such proposals depend so much on facilities that only suggestions can be given. Each teacher must consider the space and apparatus at his disposal and the time available. Fitting in with other teachers is of equal importance. In most schools, even with flexible time-tables, time in the hall, playground or field will be allocated fairly strictly. All primary-school children should have 30 minutes of physical education each day; really vigorous activity for 30 minutes is better than double this time once or twice a week. This is true even for top juniors. Allocation of time is subject to innumerable variations. It is suggested that two 30-minute lessons be allocated to games. Games lessons should not be tacked on to other physical education lessons but given over wholly to the teaching of games skills. If children are asked to concentrate at one moment on making shapes with their bodies and using balls the next, they will not accomplish either adequately. In any case, no balls should ever be allowed in a hall full of agility apparatus. Even when agility apparatus is in short supply, the teacher will court disaster if balls are allowed to roll on the floor when children are jumping, swinging or balancing. Concentration and experiment is impossible if children need to be so much aware of avoiding danger. The teacher could not anticipate or prevent situations from becoming dangerous quite suddenly.

Games lessons should be taken out of doors where more space is available than indoors, and educational gymnastics or dance lessons substituted in inclement weather. The balance of physical activities can, therefore, be restored in fine weather, subject always to space being available. This is one more reason why a class teacher should teach his own class so that this amount of flexibility is available to him. Space indoors is nearly always restricted at least in comparison with playground and field. It may well be possible for two classes to have lessons out of doors on fine days, but indoor games lessons are rarely satisfactory.

It has been suggested already that lead-up games, leading towards a variety of adult games, be arranged in units. These units are bound to be shorter for younger and longer for older children, just as the attention span of younger children is shorter than that of older ones. It is a mistake to plan to change the unit at any fixed time. So many interruptions to the ordinary time-table occur in every school that once again the teacher needs to be flexible in his planning and thinking. The weather may also make changes desirable. If the weather turns fine and warm in March, a unit planned for later in the year should be used; and if it is cold and windy in May, rounders or cricket games are quite unsuitable since even in small-side games some of the children will be fielding or waiting to bat, and thus get little activity. These games should be reserved for really warm weather.

2 *The Lesson*

Organization and methods of teaching

A.N. Whitehead in *Aims of Education*[1] says: 'The real point is to discover in practice that exact balance between freedom and discipline which will give the greatest rate of progress over the things to be known.'

In whatever neighbourhood the school is situated, 5-year-old children have much to discover when first confronted with the school's apparatus. They need freedom to choose and time to try out apparatus that is new to them. They must know they have time; they must not constantly be rushed into new experiences. But some discipline is unavoidable. Children must *always* return apparatus to the basket or receptacle it came from. Most 5-year-olds—but not all—recognize colours. Group colours are useful from the start and so are group places. The number of these depends on the number of children and the size of the baskets. Two types of organization are frequently seen:

1. All the apparatus of one kind (for example, small balls) is kept in one receptacle, and all the various receptacles are distributed along one side of the playground or field;
2. All the apparatus of different types is divided up, as far as possible according to colour, and placed in baskets.

The first organization is more obvious for reception children, but the second is more useful later on and avoids having to change the organization after a few months. The second method is advocated here. The baskets should be placed in such a position that they mark out the space to be used.

At first, infant children should be allowed to change apparatus freely and play with whatever they like. The teacher can put out all the apparatus available or put out only what he wants the children to use. He can therefore 'structure the situation'. Later, the teacher may say, for example, 'Choose a piece of apparatus you can skip with'. Later still, the teacher, perceiving the needs of his class, may specify a particular piece of apparatus. For example, 'Put the piece of apparatus you have been playing with into your baskets and take out a bat and ball; show me how

[1](Benn, 1955), p. 54.

many ways you can use your bat and ball'. The next step incorporates a brief demonstration by the teacher followed by all the children trying the same skill. After a few minutes the children go back to experimenting and playing in their own way. The lesson has begun to take the shape it will have throughout the primary school.

1 The framework of the lesson

Games lessons should start with an introductory activity followed by a skill practice, and end in a game in which the new skill or the skill just practised is applied. The teacher needs much self-discipline in coaching only those skills he has introduced or practised in the middle section of his lesson. Unless this skill is thoroughly understood and integrated in a game, coaching other skills will only confuse the children. The teacher must make a mental note of any other skills thaat need practising and include them in subsequent lessons.

An introductory activity should never be dispensed with even if time is short and the weather warm. Children, like adults, need time to adjust to the freedom of the open air, to the change of surroundings from those of the classroom, and to run about freely and with as few requirements as possible. Every child needs a piece of apparatus of his own, even at 10 years old and even in classes where discipline is easy. This is more important still where children come from restricted surroundings and strict discipline. There may be a real dilemma here. If classroom discipline is very authoritarian there is a need for children to burst out and get rid of 'excess energy'. Children do not have any excess of energy but unused energy builds up if not released and the visitor is sometimes astonished at the outbursts of a seemingly well-disciplined class. This introductory period is then very important. Indeed, the class teacher must ask himself constantly whether his handling of the children has created the need of his class to explode into movement; if so, he must give them a chance to do this.

A similar situation can arise if children have not had regular physical education lessons. The weather may have prevented outdoor lessons or the playground may have been used for dumping building materials; but whatever the reason, children must have sufficient time to adjust during the first lesson following such a period of restriction. The introductory period of this lesson should therefore be extended as long as necessary. Running games, 'release games', or dodging games may be found useful here rather than play with apparatus which might, in extreme circumstances, be treated badly. No concentration can be demanded until physical and psychological equilibrium has been restored. At the beginning of every lesson, the teacher must consider the total situation and adjust his introductory activity accordingly.

For older children the second part of the lesson requires most planning. Each skill should follow on from previous skills and lead on to the next. Much repetition is needed but this should be planned so that it does not seem exactly the same to the children. Throwing and catching can be done with the stress on the throwing action, the catching action, the length of throw or variety of throws, etc.

The skill practised in the second part of the lesson should be seen to be useful in the third part. It should be applied to a suitable game, the games like the skills following on in an orderly progression. As with the skills, the games should be played often enough to be thoroughly understood.

During the lesson, the teacher will spend a few minutes with each group, the other groups playing on their own. After the lesson the teacher will note the particular weaknesses of each group and the class as a whole, and will incorporate suitable skill practices and coaching in subsequent lessons in such a way that they fit in with his overall plan for his class.

Skill practices should be the same for the whole class. These are at first the basic skills of throwing, catching, kicking, batting, dodging, intercepting and aiming. They are then practised in the simplest situations, for example in 'Beat your own record' activities which, in turn, become skill practices for more advanced games, and the early stages of games may in turn become the skill practices of more advanced games.

2 Allocation of time

The relative length of the second and third parts of the lesson should vary with the age of the children and circumstances. The skill practice becomes gradually more important and longer: for instance, for 5-year-olds in a 20-minute lesson the skill practice may take 5 minutes. Thirty minutes may have been allocated to the games lesson but no more than 20 minutes can be considered as effective for activity, the rest of the time being taken up with changing. The skill practice should come after the children have had plenty of free-choice activities; the exact timing is immaterial. Such a lesson might be planned as follows:

Introductory activity

Free choice of apparatus from group places.

Skill practice

Beanbags: throwing and catching practice.

Teaching points: watching the beanbag rise and fall and reaching out for it.

Game

Free play with any apparatus that can be thrown and caught.

At the next stage, when the children's attention span is slightly longer, the lesson might be taken as follows:

Introductory activity

Free choice of apparatus.

Skill practice

a. Activities with hoops.

b. 'Beat your own record' activities with hoops.

Game

Free choice of apparatus or a running game.

The timing of this lesson depends on the judgement of the teacher. If the children enjoy the 'Beat your own record' activities he can set several, but allowing time for more free play at the end.

The third stage might be as follows:

Introductory activity

Free play with a piece of apparatus that can be thrown and caught.

Skill practice

a. Balls: aiming freely at targets (the targets can be lines on the playground, objects or targets on a wall, the children moving round the targets, aiming and catching their balls).

b. Choosing one target and counting aloud how many times the target can be hit; 'Beat your own record' followed by

c. Choosing a different target either with a partner or individually.

Game

Choice of apparatus for aiming.

There is no 'right' age at which these stages should be reached; it is better that progressive lessons are planned in accordance with the children's growth and development. The teacher must not hesitate to go back a stage if he thinks the children are particularly tired or excited. The length of each section cannot be laid down.

Gradually, the third part of the lesson will become more important and take up at least half the lesson, as in an educational gymnastics lesson. The introductory activity must always depend on the situation of the moment. The skill practice must neither be hurried nor unduly prolonged. If the lesson has run its course and there are a few minutes available at the end, a running game is always fun. There is no reason why traditional games such as 'tag' should not be played, provided they conform to the following conditions:

1. All the children must be able to take part
2. There is no standing about
3. The area is clearly defined
4. The game can be quickly organized
5. There are enough catchers, for example, one for every ten players
6. Each catcher can be easily distinguished from the other players.

These conditions eliminate all party-type games such as 'Grandmother's Footsteps' or 'Cat and Mouse' which have no place in a games lesson. There is a list of recommended traditional running games on pp. 142-3.

An example of a games lesson for lower juniors

Introductory activity
Free play with bat and ball or quoit, keeping on the move.

Skill practice
a. Exchanging quoits in pairs in as many ways as possible.
b. Demonstrations of correct throw, using wrist and making quoit spin in a horizontal plane; free practice of correct throw.
NOTE: one-handed catching is not demanded.
c. 'Beat your own record' activities with quoits. For example, 'How many times can you exchange your quoit while I count 10? Do this again and see if you can improve your score'.

Game
Half the class throwing quoits over a rope in pairs, making up their own rules, the other half playing French cricket 1 v. 3, or kicking tower-ball 1 v. 3.

Conclusion
A release game: four catchers for a class of forty children in a

defined area, releasing those caught by crawling between their legs. Scoring can be done in one of the following ways:

a. How many children were caught or how many children were not caught?

b. How many children did each catcher catch?

c. How many children did each player release?

An example of a games lesson for older juniors

Introductory activity

Shinty stick and ball per child; free play.

Skill practice

Skill to be taught: co-operation in attack; organization: 3 v. 2; finding some way of passing the ball between the three attacks, avoiding the defence.

Teaching points: 'Watch the position of the defence and do not hit too hard. Watch each other's position.'

Games

6 v. 6 or 4 v. 4, coaching co-operation between attacks. If enough space is available, the whole class can play shinty in appropriate lead-up games. If only one small pitch is available, either half or a quarter of the class play shinty, the other groups play basket-ball or netball-type games.

Inventing rules and scoring

Children can only invent rules, scoring and, indeed, new games if they have sufficient understanding of the possibilities. Very few people can invent in a vacuum. The wonderful inventiveness of children can only be released if the situation is prepared and limitations set. The younger the children, the narrower the limitations need to be. There is a distinction between playing freely, for example, with a ball, and making rules for a game. Free or limited choice of activity is necessary at the admission stage and frequently in introductory activities.

'Beat your own record' activities

Older infants can invent their own games in 'Beat your own record' activities. There are two main types. For example:

Type 1

a. How many ways can you find of using your ball?

Type 2

b. How high can you throw your ball and still catch it? Start throwing it a little way up and gradually throw it higher and higher.

A third type of 'Beat your own record' activities makes practices in pairs competitive (see example 'Type 3' on p. 65).

In the first type, children should find a number of ways of using a piece of apparatus, while in the second a definite skill is practised. Therefore, only the first type is useful in inducing children to use their imagination.

Making rules for a game is a more advanced stage. It can be used first when two children play together: for example, one child guards a goal, the other tries to kick a football into the goal. The children can decide how wide the goal should be or how high the ball may be kicked, or how many goals must be scored before the goalkeeper and attack change over.

In intercepting in threes or dodge-ball in threes or tower-ball, the children may make area limitations for themselves or decide when they change over. Too many rules can spoil a game.

From the 2 v. 2 stage onwards, making rules—as in all decision-making —becomes very satisfying since it can clearly make a difference to a game and affords valuable insight into a situation. But some rules can only be made by the teacher. Thus, in intercepting in threes, the teacher should, from the first introduction, insist on 'no contact'. This avoids endless conflict and makes children aware of each other from· the start. The difficulty remains of deciding who touched whom, but awareness grows as children become skilful at evasion.

As soon as children begin to play as opponents, scoring can begin. Too much should never be made of winning, but competition is a valuable motivation towards true co-operation and gives spice to a game. It is a measure, for the teacher and his pupils, in judging progress. At first, a point, a goal or a rounder is either scored or not scored. As rules get more complicated, so does the scoring. Well-known systems of scoring can be introduced, for example, as in tennis. This can be used in padder-tennis or quoit-tennis games. The badminton type of scoring is more difficult to learn but is particularly valuable with advanced top juniors. Volley-ball and deck-tennis games can be scored in this way.

Some children enjoy inventing new games. The groups need to be small and the apparatus apportioned beforehand, for example: two skittles, two canes and one large ball per group, all the groups having either the same or different apparatus. Braids and playground chalk should always be available. It is also possible to put out, for instance, baskets with assortments of balls, skittles, blocks, canes and striking implements such as shinty or hockey sticks, cricket-bat shapes, etc. (see diagrams on pp. 56 and 60) and letting groups choose their own equipment. Area limitations will then be particularly useful. These games are slower to start than set games and are not recommended for very cold or windy days. They also require a certain level of decision-making and co-operation. Sufficient time and space is another requirement. If modern methods and project work are used in the classroom, a unit of inventing games will be relatively more successful.

Penalties are a concomitant of rules and scoring. They should arise out of the game and should only be made when children can understand why they are needed. Once given, they should always be applied fairly. The more intelligent the children, the more consistent the teacher must be. Another very useful way of developing decision-making is to let children take turns at umpiring, which demands the application of rules in relation to teams and individual players. It can only be reiterated that rules, scoring and penalties must be accompanied by insight.

Tournaments

Juniors enjoy informal as well as formal tournaments. Formal tournaments are those that take place between schools, such as the 6-a-side football, circular rounders and junior netball tournaments now established in Lancashire. Groups of neighbouring junior schools run these and they are very popular with both teachers and children. In some areas junior football and netball leagues are run. How desirable are they? As has been shown elsewhere, 11-a-side teams are not necessarily bad for children of this age *provided* that children are mature enough, that coaching takes place out of school time and that undue importance is not attached to matches. But these provisos are most important. The majority of children cannot possibly cope with adult techniques or tactics, and the excitement, sense of failure and/or hero-worship at too young an age that often follows. Some teachers feel that even small-side tournaments engender the wrong attitudes among children and adults, but the friendly atmosphere and careful matching of teams from different-sized schools can eliminate much of the stress common in adult sport.

Informal tournaments successfully finish off a unit of games. They can be played from the 4-a-side stage onwards. Only American tournaments are recommended, which give each team an opportunity to play against several other teams. Not more than three or four teams should play each other. Supposing there were thirty-two children in the class, two sets of four teams could compete, the winners playing each other. The diagram shows two types of chart for keeping the score.

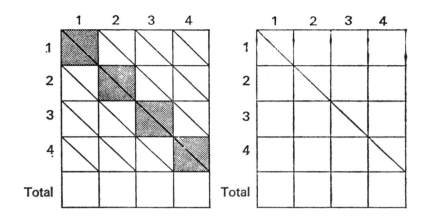

Order of play

Each team's score will be put into the top triangle of each square, the other team's score in the lower triangle. Add up all top triangle scores or any team's total.	The scores of each team are marked opposite the number of the team against which the score has been made. Add up each team's score.

Team 1 v. Team 2
,,   1 v.   ,,   3
,,   1 v.   ,,   4
,,   2 v.   ,,   3
,,   2 v.   ,,   4
,,   3 v.   ,,   4

For padder-tennis and quoit-tennis, tournaments can be played when the children can use the usual rules and scoring. The teacher and the children can make the rules together and vary them from official rules as required. The rules for the tournaments can be put up in the classroom together with a chart for scoring. In this way, agreed rules will be used.

Rules to be agreed on must include:

1. The length of the match and half-time or how a set is to be determined as, for example, in padder-tennis
2. Who umpires
3. How ends are to be chosen
4. Scoring and who keeps the score
5. Area, equipment and safety
6. Playing rules.

Tournaments should never be dragged out. They should be completed in two lessons at most. If the weather imposes an interruption of more than a week, the tournament should either be restarted or dropped.

The teacher should choose the teams in each section. He must use his judgement so as to be fair to the best and least capable teams. If two sets of teams play each other, the two best teams should be put into different sets. If scoring is, for example, by goals, not wins, the poorest teams must also be separated so that an average team does not accumulate too many points against two poor ones. This procedure of 'seeding' may seem unfair until one reflects what would happen if the teams were simply drawn out of a hat. All the best teams might then be in the same set and would eliminate each other. When the winners of each set came to play each other, the match could be very uneven. If, on the other hand, the class is already divided into a 6-a-side and 4-a-side teams, two separate tournaments are best.

Apparatus

Generally speaking, the more apparatus a school possesses the better. It should be kept in one central stock and each teacher should have equal access. One teacher needs to be in charge to see that balls are regularly blown up, braids stitched, stores kept tidy, and that some equipment is kept in reserve. Some schools divide up all games equipment and each teacher is in charge of his allocation. This means, invariably, that each class has too little for effective teaching. Great care and co-operation among staff is vital even in the best equipped schools. If sufficient care is taken, then all equipment need not be replaced each year and new types of apparatus can be bought.

1 *Games equipment for infant schools*

All equipment should be stored on a four-basket trolley or on two three-basket trolleys for four or six groups respectively.

Here is a recommended supply of apparatus to serve a class of about forty children:

1 small rubber ball per child and/or tennis ball or tennis core ball
1 air-flow ball per child (2½″, 3½″, or 5″ diameter)
1 large ball per child, strong enough to kick (half the class to have size 3 and half to have size 4 balls)
1 bat (3 or 4 ply) per child (see diagram, p. 56)
1 beanbag per child
1 skipping rope per child
1 block or skittle (stackable ones are useful) per child
1 quoit per child
1 hoop per child

1 cane per child
8 posts with firm bases
playground chalk
coloured braids (preferably one for each child in the school)

2 *Games equipment for junior schools*

All small equipment should be stored on one four-basket trolley or on two three-basket trolleys. The following supply of apparatus is recommended for a class of about thirty-six children:

1 small rubber or tennis ball per child
1 size 4 ball per child, strong enough for all purposes (or half the class to have size 4 and half to have size 5 balls)
1 hoop per child, half the number to be 24 inches and half 36 inches
1 cane (4 feet) per child
1 braid or bib per child
1 padder-tennis bat between two or,
1 short tennis racket between two
1 skipping rope between two
1 cricket-bat shape between two
1 rounders stick between two
1 shinty stick between two
1 light hockey stick between two
18 stumps
4 stool-ball bats
8 basket-balls (strong moulded plastic or rubber)
8 volley-balls or light plastic balls size 4 (these must not be kicked)
12 all-purpose posts with firm bases, preferably high enough to allow for: padder-tennis (net at waist-height);[1] quoit games (net at shoulder-height); rounders (4', 4'6"); volley-ball (net just above reach-height)
1 skittle or cone between two
4 stool-ball posts
4 netball posts (these may be used for volley-ball)
padder-tennis, quoit tennis and volley-ball nets if the school is affluent, otherwise skipping ropes
repair kits
pump with adaptor for balls with valves
whistles
playground chalk
1 measuring tape

[1]These approximate heights are related to the children.

Summary of recommendations in chapters 1 and 2

1. The class teacher should teach his own class in primary-school games lessons.
2. Correct techniques should be taught from the beginning.
3. Techniques should be taught complete at first, details later.
4. Only correct techniques should be demonstrated.
5. Tactical situations should be built up from easy to complex ones.
6. Similarities and differences in games should be pointed out. Two very similar games should not be started at the same time.
7. Games should suit the physical, intellectual, psychological and moral stage of development of groups of children.
8. Rules, scoring and penalties should only be taught if they can be fully understood.
9. Adult games should only be attempted by exceptional children as extra-curricular activities.
10. Special allowances should be given to schools in poor neighbourhoods for clothing and equipment.
11. Both the teacher and the children should change for games lessons.

3   *Choice of Lesson Material*

The reader will need to choose carefully from the following lesson material, bearing in mind all the considerations outlined in chapters 1 and 2. It is not possible to allocate lesson material to specific age groups or 'infants' or 'juniors'. In some areas children change schools at 7 years, in others at 8 years; and where the recommendations of the Plowden Report are being implemented, a change of schools at 9 is likely. A change of schools should not lead to a break in the continuity of teaching. It is far more important to choose lesson material which is right for a particular class and conditions. Even then, the same game or the same stage of a lead-up game is highly unlikely to suit all the children in a class, especially those taught in family units. 'Individual differences between children of the same age are so great that any class, however homogeneous it seems, must always be treated as a body of children needing individual and different attention.'[1]

It is often necessary, even with much older children, to start with the simplest skills when a new game is taught. Most teachers will revise the basic skills of a game before playing the next stage in a progression of lead-up games the following season. It is highly desirable that children should have as great a variety of skills as possible at their command, that they should play many different games and learn them—as far as the teacher is able to give them the opportunity—at the best possible moment. It is also obvious and indeed desirable that many teachers and children will play games beyond the scope of this book.

A reference to relay races was made on p. 18. Relay races were very popular in the past especially where equipment was scarce. Why is there no section on relay races in this book? The following reasons make relay races undesirable in an educational context.

1. Only one child is occupied in each team, the others are getting cold or over-excited.
2. The shy, the clumsy, the emotionally unstable child goes through agonies trying not to let his team down.

[1] *Children and their Primary Schools* (HMSO, 1967), par. 75a.

3. The large, the speedy, the well co-ordinated child is likely to do well without any great effort on his part.
4. There is no decision-making process involved.
5. Skills must necessarily be extremely simple.
6. Emotionally charged situations are engendered which cannot find an adequate outlet.
7. Concentration in a setting of excitement is very difficult.
8. Even the simplest skills tend to break down: balls are dropped, skipping ropes get entangled, hoops clatter on the floor.

In situations where the educational aspects of skill-learning, decision-making, adaptation to a variety of situations and finding many different responses are not important, relay races have their place and can be great fun.

Small apparatus activities

1 *Individual activities*

Individual activities are concerned with small apparatus. These activities may be played with infants but many will be found applicable in the preliminary stages of games or as introductory activities or to coach a specific basic skill. No attempt has been made to put the following activities in order of difficulty.

Small rubber or tennis balls

Under-arm throwing—general teaching points:

a. Stance: transferring the weight from the back foot to the front foot which is opposite to the hand with the ball.
b. Releasing the ball by opening the fingers suddenly.
c. Following through, extending the wrist and elbow in the direction of the throw.
d. Finding out which hand is the most comfortable to use, and practising with either.

Teaching points for over-arm throwing will be found under 'Activities in pairs', p. 63-4.

Catching—general teaching points:

a. Observing the rise and fall of the ball and moving towards it.
b. Extending and spreading the fingers in the direction of the fall of the ball.
c. Putting the heels of the palms together.

d. Closing the fingers round the ball and bringing the hands together towards the chest.

e. Going with the whole body in the direction of the fall of the ball.

Bouncing—general teaching points:

a. Letting the ball fall.

b. Increasing the pressure with the hands to make it bounce.

c. Observing the direction of the bounce and moving in the direction of the rise of the ball to catch it.

Some other activities with small balls:

a. Batting.

b. Rolling the ball on the ground and fielding it.

c. Throwing from one hand to the other.

d. Throwing against a wall and catching on the rebound or after one bounce.

Variations can be made along these lines: one or both hands, direction, level, on the spot, moving. Further practice can be given with 'Beat your own record' activities. For example:

Type 1

a. How many different ways can you use your ball?

b. In how many different directions can you throw your ball and run after it and catch it?

c. Can you make holes with your body and the ground, and throw your ball or roll it through them?

Type 2

a. How high can you throw your ball?

b. Start throwing your ball a little way up and catch it; then throw it a little higher and catch it; keep throwing it a little higher each time until you drop it. Then start again and see if you can throw it higher the next time.

c. Throw your ball a little way ahead and run after it and catch it; keep moving until you drop your ball. Then try again and see if you can go on longer this time.

d. Bounce your ball a little way ahead, run after it and catch it; keep moving until you drop it. Then try again and see if you can continue longer this time.

e. Roll your ball, run after it and field it.

Further 'Beat your own record' activities can be concerned with speed, stopping and starting, height, direction, length and gesture. For example, 'Clap your hands once, twice, etc., while the ball is in the air'.

Bats and balls

Bats must have handles that are narrow and long enough for children to hold comfortably. They must be strong enough for vigorous hitting and light enough so that small children can continue playing for several minutes. For older children, bats must be stronger and heavier. The range of polypropylene bats now available allows the provision of a selection of bats which are both light and strong. Short tennis rackets in hardwearing plastic for use with a light-weight ball are a useful addition to equipment.

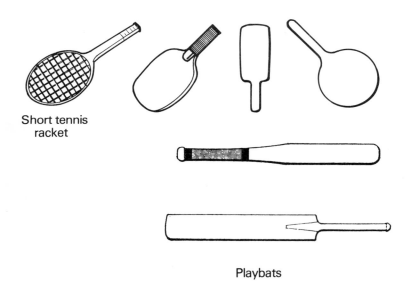

Short tennis
racket

Playbats

Use of bats and balls—teaching points:

a. Hitting with the centre of the bat.

b. Keeping the bat well away from the body.

c. Observing the ball's rise and fall.

d. Looking at the ball, not the bat, and getting the 'feel' of the distance between the body and the bat.

e. Keeping the feet moving in the direction of the ball.

Different balls can be used with playbats:
air-flow balls;
rubber or tennis balls or tennis core balls.

'Beat your own record' activities:

Type 1

a. How many different ways can you use your bat and ball? (The teacher must decide if batting cricket-style is permissible, as the tip of the bat may scrape the ground.)

b. How fast or in how many different directions or how many times can you hit your ball?

c. How many different balls can you use?

Large balls

Size 2, 3 or 4 in rubber or plastic, preferably in team colours. Balls must be strong enough for vigorous throwing, hitting a target or kicking. This applies especially to the larger balls.

Teaching points

As for small balls, but using fingers, not palms, for catching.

'Beat your own record' activities:

Type 1

a. How many different ways can you throw your ball?

b. How many different ways can you use your ball, keeping it on the ground?

c. How many different ways can you keep your ball up in the air?

Type 2

a. Throw your ball a little way in the air and catch it. Throw it a little higher and catch it. Keep throwing it higher each time until you drop it, then start again and see if you can throw it higher the next time.

b. Dribble your ball and see if you can keep it near your feet.

c. Bounce your ball a little way ahead, run after it and catch it; keep moving until you drop it, then try again and see if you can continue longer this time.

d. Keep running round the playground and bounce your ball on all the crosses or lines that you see (chalk marks or existing lines).

Aiming with balls

This is a stage of development which follows after a certain amount of skill in manipulating a ball has been reached. It can be practised against a wall, but where no wall is available it is better practised in pairs (see 'Aiming at targets', pp. 66-8).

Beanbags

Beanbags are harder for small hands to release but easier to catch than balls as they are pliable and even a corner of them may give sufficient hold for catching. They may be made of bright colours and thus easier to see than dull or dark coloured balls. Catching with both hands should be coached at first, but children will soon find out that one hand can reach farther than both and that beanbags are 'easy' to catch with one hand. Teaching points for throwing and catching are the same as for small rubber balls. Activities include: throwing and catching in different directions, round, under and between parts of the body, on the spot but not standing still, and on the move. 'Beat your own record' activities can include both finding different ways of throwing and catching and throwing at different heights or with more or less force, and using either or both hands and in different directions. Beanbags can also be used for aiming and are at first better than balls in this respect as they do not roll away; for example, aiming the beanbag into a hoop and moving farther and farther away. Other targets could be lines, braids, skittles or blocks, other beanbags, or a coil or shape made with a skipping rope.

The teacher and the children will find many 'Beat your own record' activities:

Type 1

a. How many different ways can you throw and catch your beanbag?
b. How many ways can you find of throwing the beanbag round a part of your body?
c. How many different ways can you find of using your right and your left hand?

Type 2

a. Throw your beanbag a little way in the air. If you catch it, throw it a little higher. How high can you throw your beanbag and still catch it?
b. Throw your beanbag in the air and clap once, catch it, throw it up again and clap twice. See how many times you can clap, throwing and catching your beanbag.
c. Throw your beanbag a little way ahead and catch it. Now throw it a little farther ahead and keep throwing it farther ahead. See how fast you can run, throwing and catching your beanbag.

Skipping ropes

Both boys and girls enjoy skipping and will practise for relatively long times to learn to skip. Where boys think skipping is cissy it is a sure sign the activity is 'culture-bound', that is to say, that in the neighbourhood and/or in the school, girls' and boys' activities are separated and different behaviour is expected from boys and girls. The teacher will soon get over this if he can find a photograph of some well-known boxer practising skipping.

Skipping ropes should be long enough to hang just above the ankles when held with the arms outstretched. Bound ends are best but a knot will do. Handles are a nuisance if the rope is to be used for other purposes such as tying to posts or as a target.

Children can skip forward and backward, slower and faster, on the spot and moving. They can invent many steps once the basic skill has been mastered, and later they enjoy skipping in groups. Some children have a great store of skipping rhymes.

'Beat your own record' activities:

Type 1
a. In how many different directions can you turn your skipping rope?
b. How many different steps can you think of which make you move forward with your skipping rope?
c. How many different steps can you invent while skipping?
d. Make a shape with your skipping rope on the ground. How many ways can you find of jumping over it?

Type 2
a. How fast can you turn your skipping rope or how slowly?
b. How high can you skip while turning your rope?

Blocks or skittles

Skittles can be 12 inches, 18 inches or 24 inches in height. Blocks are usually 12 inches by 2 inches by 2 inches. There are numerous ways in which blocks can be built up, and they are best used as obstacles for jumping over or as targets or to mark a goal or area. They need to have an indentation at both ends to hold a cane.

Although jumping activities are not always associated with games, they are fun for small children and excellent for use in cold weather.

Skittles can be plain or extendable or stackable. There are several types and shapes. Like blocks, they should have an indentation at the top to hold a cane. Extensions made of wood tend to break and are not recommended. Some types have metal rods in the centre which are an improvement on the wooden ones. The newest stackable plastic skittle (available in four colours and various heights) is very stable in windy weather and can be used with a cane for jumping over, or extended by inserting a pole. Skittles or cones can also become targets, or be used to mark a goal or area.

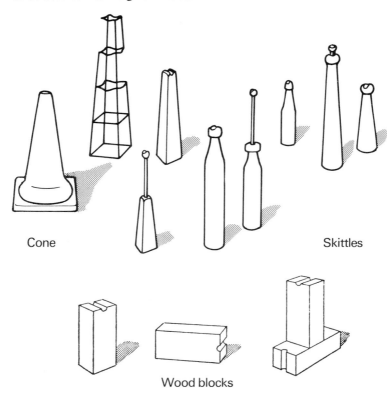

Cone   Skittles

Wood blocks

'Beat your own record' activities include:

Type 1
a. How many different ways can you build up your blocks and still jump over them?
b. Can you arrange your blocks in different ways on the ground and find different ways of jumping over them?

Type 2
a. How high can you extend your skittle and still jump over the cane?
b. How far away from your skittle can you be and still hit it with your beanbag or ball?

Hoops

There should be a selection of 24-inch and 36-inch hoops for smaller and taller children. Hoops are useful for several reasons. They can be used as a piece of apparatus in their own right but also to keep balls or group equipment in place or to mark an area as, for example, in a rounders game; or they may be used as a target. Infants enjoy jumping from one hoop to another. They can put the hoops in a pattern on the ground and vary the pattern in lots of ways. Other examples of uses are: bowling, hula-hooping, skipping, spinning and running round the hoop.

Examples of 'Beat your own record' activities for hoops:

Type 1

a. How many ways can you find of moving from one hoop to another?

b. How many ways can you find of moving in and out of your hoop using both your hands and your feet?

Type 2

a. How long can you continue bowling your hoop without bumping into anyone?

b. How long can you continue bowling your hoop using left and right hands, changing from one side of your hoop to the other?

c. Can you bowl your hoop so that you can run right round it while it is moving?

d. Spin your hoop, leave it and run and touch a line, then run back and catch your hoop before it drops. Now move farther from the line and try again. See how far you can get from the line, spinning and catching your hoop before it drops.

e. Bowl your hoop, jump through it and catch it again before it falls.

f. Bowl your hoop, run to face it and jump over it, or jump from side to side of your hoop.

Quoits

Rubber quoits are best. They should be smooth, easy to hold and not too thick. Their main use is for throwing and catching, but they can also be aimed at a target and make a good variation on balls for such games as intercepting in threes. In individual work the correct throw for quoit- or deck-tennis cannot be practised since it depends on distance from an opponent, but children can get used to the feel of the ring and the hold for catching. They should be encouraged to catch with their fingers and palms and to use two hands at first.

Examples of 'Beat your own record' activities:

a. Throw your quoit a little way ahead and run and catch it. See how far ahead you can throw your quoit and still catch it.

b. How high can you throw your quoit and catch it?

Canes

Canes on their own can be used to mark a space or as obstacles for jumping. More often they are used in conjunction with blocks and skittles, for jumping over and crawling under. They can be used in series, and children find many ways of arranging them.

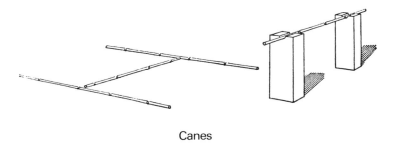

Canes

'Beat your own record' activities:

Type 1

Choose a way of arranging your canes and then find as many ways of getting over them as you can.

Type 2

a. Use your cane as a starting line: run and jump as far forward as you can. Mark the spot behind your heels and start again.

b. Arrange your cane on your blocks or skittles and jump over it.

c. Extend your skittles gradually and see how high you can jump.

Playground chalk

This has very many uses, especially on a playground without any markings. Children can mark lines or other shapes for jumping over or for use as targets. They can use the chalk to show how far they have jumped or to mark a starting line or an area. Another use of playground chalk is for marking out circles. This can be done quite easily if one child holds the end of a skipping rope in position, the other holds the chalk and the taut skipping rope and walks backwards; a circle will result.

'Beat your own record' activities:

Type 1

a. How many different targets can you draw and then throw or bounce and catch your ball round them?

b. How many ways can you find of jumping over your shapes?

Type 2

a. Draw two lines and jump over them. Draw another line farther away and see if you can jump over all three. How far can you jump, putting your lines farther and farther away from the first?

b. Bounce your ball along all the straight lines you can see on the playground.

c. Look at all the chalk circles on the playground. See how many circles you can bounce your ball round while I count 10.

2 Activities in pairs

This apparatus is particularly useful:
balls
bats and balls
beanbags
quoits.
The main skills are:
throwing
catching
kicking
aiming.

The following activities are still concerned with the handling of apparatus but now in relation to another child. All the above apparatus can be exchanged in a variety of ways and children should find as many as possible by themselves. It is assumed that by the time children play in pairs they are familiar with the basic throwing, catching, kicking and aiming actions except for these two:
correct over-arm throwing with small balls;
correct quoit throwing.

Correct over-arm throwing with small balls—teaching points:

a. Extending the elbow backward about shoulder height and *well away from the body.*

b. Holding the ball between the fingers, not in the palm.

c. Transferring the weight from the back foot to the front foot, using opposite foot and hand.

d. A quick extension of the elbow, wrist and fingers in that order, in the direction of the flight of the ball; noting the outward twist in the wrist.

e. Following through with the whole body and extended arm, wrist and fingers.

Bad habits most often seen:
elbow tucked into side
wrist stiff
no follow through.

Correct quoit throwing—teaching points:

a. Hold the quoit flat.

b. Bend the wrist and elbow towards the body, fingers spread out.

c. Put the same foot forward as the hand holding the quoit.

d. Shift the weight from the back foot to the front foot at the same time as the elbow and wrist is suddenly and energetically extended in the direction of the throw.

e. A quoit should fly flat and not wobble.

'Beat your own record' activities, using balls, bats and balls, beanbags and quoits:

Type 1

a. How many ways can you find of exchanging your apparatus?

b. How many ways can you find of exchanging your apparatus by throwing it over, under or between parts of your body?

c. How many ways can you throw or hit or kick your apparatus so that your partner is forced to move in order to retrieve it?

d. Exchange your apparatus in two alternate ways so that you can feel the rhythm.

e. How many ways can you find of exchanging your apparatus while moving?

Type 2

Two children co-operating with each other.

a. Start close to your partner, exchanging your ball, move farther and farther apart until you drop your ball.

b. Use one of the following ways of exchanging your ball, moving farther and farther apart: over-arm throwing, under-arm throwing, under-arm bowling, kicking, rolling.

c. Exchange your ball and move one step apart each time you catch it. Move one step forward each time you drop it.

d. Exchange your ball on the move and count the number of exchanges while I count 10. Now do it again and see if you can improve your own record.

Type 3

Two children competing with each other.

a. No. 1 throw and catch or bounce and catch your ball, beanbag or quoit; no. 2 try to intercept it. Count interceptions.
b. No. 1 keep one foot in a chalk circle and try the same game. (NOTE: only the ball may be touched, not the other child. This is the first appearance of the 'no contact' rule.)

Teaching points

The child in possession of the ball should twist and turn and play it high or low; the interceptor should reach well out and bat or pat the ball with the finger-tips.

c. No. 1 dribble the ball, no. 2 intercept using feet only.
d. No. 1 use basket-ball technique, that is, dribbling with one hand only, finger-tips only touching the ball; no. 2 intercept. (NOTE: *c.* and *d.* can have an area limitation.)
e. How many times can you throw or hit or kick your ball or other apparatus so that your partner is forced to move to return it? Count a point every time you make your partner move about; remember it is no use throwing or hitting your ball or quoit where he cannot possibly reach it.

Bats and balls

'Beat your own record' activities:

a. Using bats and air-flow balls, how many times can you exchange your ball without dropping it?
b. Using bats and rubber balls, find the best distance for exchanging your ball and keep exchanging it. Count the number of hits in the rally and try to improve each time. The ball may bounce once or twice.
c. Using padder-tennis bats and rubber or tennis balls, how long a rally can you keep up without dropping the ball? Your ball may bounce once or twice. You may also hit the ball before it bounces.

Beanbags

'Beat your own record' activities:

Type 1

a. How many ways can you find of exchanging your beanbag?

b. How many ways can you find of throwing your beanbag to your partner under, over or between parts of your body?

c. How many ways can you exchange your beanbag while on the move?

Type 2

a. No. 1 throw your beanbag in the air; if no. 2 catches it he throws it up. Count how many times each of you can catch and throw the beanbag.

b. How many times can you exchange your beanbag, throwing underarm while on the move, before you drop it?

c. How far apart can you move while throwing and catching your beanbag?

Quoits

'Beat your own record' activities:

Type 1

a. How many ways can you exchange your quoit using either one or both hands to catch?

b. How many ways can you throw your quoit under, over or between different parts of your body?

Type 2

a. How many times can you exchange your quoit, keeping it moving without wobbling?

b. Count the number of times you can exchange your quoit, catching with one hand.
(NOTE: the children can agree on scoring, for example: one point for two-handed catch, two points for catching with the right hand, three points for catching with the left hand.)

c. Count the number of times you can throw with the hand with which you caught the quoit.

Aiming at targets.

Skills with balls, bats and balls, beanbags and quoits can be used for aiming. The children can agree on rules and targets.

Targets on the ground

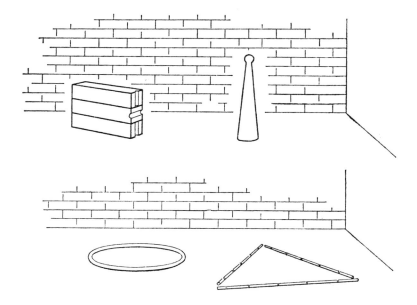

1. Two blocks or skittles, preferably against a wall or fence, marking a goal. One child guards the goal, the other tries to kick or throw the ball between goal-posts. The children can decide the width of the goal, when to change over and how to score.

2. A skittle between two children. The children can increase their distance from the skittle, aiming their ball at knocking it down.

3. Two skittles, the children on either side. The ball must be rolled between the two skittles. The children can decide on the distance between the skittles and scoring.

4. Lines, shapes or hoops on the ground. Existing lines can be used or shapes can be marked with playground chalk or hoops can be used, or skipping ropes can be dropped so that they make irregular shapes.

   The children hit their target in turn, increasing their distance. They can choose from beanbags, balls or quoits.

5. One child bounces the ball in his target, his partner catching. He can either bounce from side to side or run round his target. They bounce the ball alternately and continuously in and round the target.

Targets on a wall

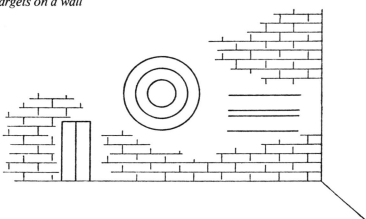

For each target different apparatus and skills are required. Both teacher and children can think of many variations of the following activities:

1. Under-arm throwing in pairs, aiming at circles. The children take it in turns to throw and decide on rules about scoring. Different kinds of balls can be used.
2. Cricket bowling practice, using lines on the wall as a wicket. The children can agree on the bowling action, over-arm and under-arm, the distance from the target and the rules for scoring.
3. Using bats and balls and a single line 65 centimetres above the floor. The ball should be hit above the line and the children should hit alternately. They can decide on the distance from the target, whether or not a bounce is allowed, and scoring. In addition, rules may have to be made about the area to be used if several couples are playing.

Activities over nets or ropes

The correct heights of the nets for padder-tennis, deck-tennis and volley-ball are respectively 65 centimetres (72 centimetres at the posts), 1.23 metres and 2.43 metres (2.24 metres for girls). A rough guide for the teacher is the children's waist-height, shoulder-height and reach-height. There is no real need for nets: skipping ropes are quite sufficient at first. They should be white, to show up well. Posts must be strong enough so that the nets or ropes can be tied firmly and there is no 'sag', especially on windy days. Any kind of post will do: for example, netball posts, rounders posts, jumping stands or improvised posts. A tin can with a fixed lid can be filled with sand and a sturdy post fitted through a hole in the lid. Nets or ropes can also be attached to hooks on a wall at one side.

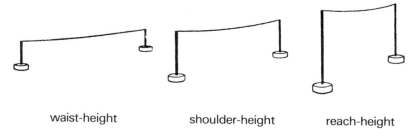

waist-height   shoulder-height   reach-height

Posts with ropes

Net at waist-height

Suggested apparatus per pair:
    palm and rubber ball or tennis core ball
    light-weight playbat each and air-flow ball
    stronger playbat each and rubber or tennis ball
    padder-tennis bat each and tennis ball
    beanbag

Net at shoulder-height

Suggested apparatus per pair:
    large ball
    beanbag
    quoit
    light-weight bat each and shuttlecock
    badmington racket each and shuttlecock   } if ability allows

Net at reach-height

Suggested apparatus per pair:
    large light-weight ball size 4
    volley ball
    beanbag

No area limitation is needed at first unless pairs of children interfere with each other. The teacher should remember that co-operation is required of the children at this stage. It is far more useful to teach co-operation than to force competition before the children can thoroughly cope with all the new skills in pairs. If 'Beat your own record' activities are used, they will be motivation enough. The teacher should beware of asking questions of the class which make some children cock-sure and others despondent. 'Who beat their own record?' is better than 'Who played the longest rally?' In any case, at the age when play in pairs can first be introduced the majority of children will not answer truthfully.

Net at waist-height

'Beat your own record' activities:

Type 1

a. How many ways can you find of exchanging your ball over the net, using your palms to hit with?
b. How many ways can you find of exchanging your air-flow ball, using a small bat?
c. How many ways can you exchange a beanbag over the net?

Type 2

a. Hit your rubber ball across the net with your open palm. Count how long a rally you can keep up. Try to keep it up longer each time.

Teaching points

   i. Keep your hand flat, firm but not stiff.
  ii. Look first at the ball before it bounces, then where you are aiming it.
 iii. Decide if you wish to let it bounce once or twice.

b. Hit your air-flow ball so that it does not bounce. See how long you can keep it going.

Teaching points

  i. Use quick, light hits.
 ii. Keep your wrist supple.

c. Count how many times you can hit a tennis ball with your padder-tennis bat on the right and on the left side of you.

Teaching points

   i. Turn your whole body to the right or left.
  ii. Swing your whole arm and hit really hard.
 iii. Decide if you want the ball to bounce once or twice.

d. How many ways can you throw your beanbag so that your partner needs to move to catch it?

Teaching points

i. Look at your partner's eyes and hands and guess where the beanbag is going to go.
ii. Throw it so that it is possible for your partner to catch it if he moves.

Net at shoulder-height

'Beat your own record' activities:

Type 1
a. How many ways can you find of exchanging your ball across the net?

Teaching points

i. Think of different ways of holding the ball, such as overhead, at shoulder-height, at chest-height and low.
ii. Think of high and low passes.
iii. Think of places on both sides of your partner to where you can throw.

b. In how many different ways can you exchange either a beanbag or a quoit?

Teaching points

i. Think of the different sides from which your partner can catch.
ii. Think how high your partner could jump to catch.
iii. Think how close to the net or how far away you could be for throwing and catching.
iv. Reach out with either hand as far as you can for catching.
v. Decide if you will allow catching with both hands or only one.

c. Find out how many ways you can hit the shuttlecock

Teaching points

i. Always keep your wrist supple.
ii. Turn from side to side to hit.
iii. Hold the shuttlecock by the neck, not the top, and let it go vertically.

Type 2

a. How far away from the net can you stand and still throw and catch your ball, beanbag or quoit? Move towards the net if you drop it; move farther away if you catch it.

Teaching points

   i. Decide if one- or two-handed catches are allowed.
  ii. Move towards the ball, beanbag or quoit as soon as you see where it is going to go.
 iii. See if you can manage to throw the beanbag or quoit with the same hand you used for catching.

b. See how many times you can hit your shuttlecock with your bat or racket to each side of your partner (if ability allows).

Teaching points

   i. Hold your bat or racket with your wrist supple, but firm (not stiff).
  ii. Reach out high or low to hit.
 iii. Keep on your toes so that you can run quickly, sideways or forward or backward.
 iv. Do not let the shuttlecock touch the ground.
  v. Try to hit the shuttlecock close to the net or farther back so that your partner needs to run about on his side of the net.

c. See how much you can make your partner run about on his side of the net, using any apparatus.

Teaching points

   i. Vary your throw or hit, for example: high, low, close to or far away from the net.
  ii. Be prepared to run anywhere on your side of the net to catch or hit.
 iii. Look closely at your partner at the moment when he throws or hits, then move to where you think the ball, beanbag or quoit will fall.
 iv. Consider it a bad throw or hit if your partner does not need to move from his spot to catch the object.
  v. Throw from the position in which you caught the apparatus.

Net at reach-height

'Beat your own record' activities:

Type 1

a. Throw your ball or beanbag over the net in as many ways as you can think of. Count how many different types of throw you can find.

Teaching points

   i. Catch your ball with both hands or your beanbag with one or both hands.

  ii. Reach out and jump to catch.

 iii. Do not let the ball or beanbag touch the ground.

 iv. Do not fling the ball or beanbag but throw properly with one or two hands.

  v. Throw high, low, to either side or close to or far away from the net.

b. See how much you can make your partner run about on his side of the net. Try to make him run even farther every time you throw.

Teaching points

   i. Think as you catch where you intend to throw the ball next.

  ii. Guess where the ball will drop by observing your partner's eyes and hands and judge the flight of the ball.

 iii. Keep on your toes so that you can change direction swiftly.

 iv. Reach out and jump high to catch.

  v. Decide whether you must throw from the position in which you caught the ball or if you may move.

Type 2

a. Count how many times you can throw your ball over the net without dropping it.

(NOTE: the ball is still thrown and caught, not volleyed as in volleyball.)

b. Use a beanbag and make up a game of throwing and catching over the high net.

Hoops

'Beat your own record' activities:

Type 1

a. No. 1 hold the hoop in various ways: horizontally, vertically, at an angle. No. 2 find as many different ways as possible of getting from one side of the hoop to the other.

Teaching points

   i. No. 1 hold your hoop still while your partner is moving; use two hands.

   ii. Think of the next position in which you will hold your hoop.

   iii. No. 2 think of lots of different ways of jumping or crawling through, over, under and round the hoops. Go backwards or sideways or with different parts of your body leading. Try putting your hands in the hoop and jumping your feet from side to side. Always think ahead of the next move.

   iv. Decide when to change over: for example, after every three jumps.

b. No. 1 hold two hoops in various ways, making it as difficult as possible for your partner to get through both of them.

c. Arrange several hoops on the ground in any pattern you like. Play 'Follow My Leader' in and out and over the hoops.

Teaching points

   i. Place your hoops so that they do not get in other children's way.

   ii. Decide when to change over.

d. No. 1 bowl your hoop. No. 2 find as many ways of jumping through or over it as you can while the hoop is moving.

Type 2

a. Spin your hoop and run and pick up your partner's hoop before it drops. Start fairly close together and increase your distance with every turn.

Teaching points

   i. Hold the hoop vertically, with your thumb bent over your fingers.

   ii. Use as much pressure as possible when spinning the hoop.

b. Spin your hoop, run round your partner's and back to your own before it drops. Increase the distance between your hoops.

c. No. 1 bowl your hoop. No. 2 choose one particular way of getting over the hoop while it is moving. Practise this until you can do it every time.

Teaching points

    i. No. 2 think of the way you should take off for your jump and how soon you should jump.

    ii. Consider whether you should stand facing the hoop or at the side of the hoop.

    iii. Think before you jump how high you need to lift your legs.

    iv. Decide when to change over.

d. No. 1 hold your hoop well away from your body standing on a box or a chair. No. 2 run and throw your ball through the hoop and catch it on the other side.

Teaching points

    i. No. 1 hold your hoop quite still while No. 2 is running.

    ii. No. 1 you may change the position of your hoop after every successful throw and catch.

    iii. Decide when to change over.

e. Place your hoop on the ground between you and bounce the ball in the hoop. Increase your distance from the hoop. Use over-arm throws.

f. Aim at a skittle in your hoop and see if you can knock it over. Change sides after each successful throw.

g. Bounce a ball in your hoop while running round it.

Teaching points

    i. Use either hand for throwing and catch with both hands.

    ii. No. 1 call 'Change' and both of you change direction.

    iii. Keep sideways to the hoop, do *not* use slip steps.

Canes

'Beat your own record' activities:

    Type 1

a. No. 1 hold the cane. No. 2 jump over it in as many ways as you can think of.

Teaching points

    i. Do not jump so that your feet might kick your partner's face.

    ii. Decide when to change over.

b. No. 1 hold two canes in different ways. No. 2 find several ways of either jumping over them in turn or in one jump.

c. Place several canes on the ground and play 'Follow My Leader'.

Type 2

Draw two lines several yards apart on the ground. No. 1 take off behind line 'A' and jump as far forward as possible, landing on two feet. No. 2 place a cane behind your partner's heels. No. 1 jump again, taking off *behind* the cane. See how few jumps you need to get from line 'A' to line 'B', using two canes alternately as jumping-off cane and marker. Change over.

Teaching points

i. Decide if you want to use a standing or running jump.
ii. Place the cane behind the back heel if you are not landing with both feet together.
iii. Try hopping.

(NOTE: the distance between 'A' and 'B' should be shorter.)

Shinty sticks

'Beat your own record' activities:

Type 1

a. Use the three jumping games you played over canes.
b. Each of you hold one round and one straight end of two shinty sticks. Climb in and out of the shinty sticks and your partner's legs without letting go.

Teaching points

i. Start forward or sideways or backward.
ii. Hold the shinty sticks tightly.

Type 2

See 'Beat your own record' activities with canes, above.

Skipping ropes

'Beat your own record' activities:

Type 1

a. No. 1 skip with the skipping rope. No. 2 find several ways of joining No. 1: e.g., face your partner or turn your back on him.
b. Each of you hold one end of the skipping rope, turn it and either skip at the same time or find some way of turning under and round it without losing the rhythm.
c. Place one or more skipping ropes on the ground, either tied or loose, and play 'Follow My Leader'. Change over.

Playground chalk

'Beat your own record' activities:

Type 1

a. Mark a series of shapes on the ground and jump over them with your feet together. Play 'Follow My Leader'.

Teaching points

  i. Decide how you will change over.

  ii. Play this hopping; change over when the leader puts two feet on the ground.

b. Invent a game similar to hop-scotch.

Type 2

a. Draw a shape on the ground and stand on either side of it. Bounce your ball into the shape and increase your distance from it.

b. Mark a line or shape as a target and aim at it with a beanbag. Increase your distance.

c. Draw two lines on the ground. Your partner must take off behind line 'A' and when he lands you mark a line behind his heels. He must use this line as his next starting line. Count the jumps he needs to get from line 'A' to line 'B'. Then try to beat him, your partner drawing the lines behind your heels.

(See also 'Targets on the ground' p. 67, and activities with canes, pp. 75-6.)

4   *Progressions of Lead-up Games and Skill Practices*

The following progressions of lead-up games show the building-up of the most usual primary-school games; each stage is consecutively wider in scope and complexity. There are suggestions for rules to be made by the teacher either for reasons of safety or to ensure good organization; outlines are also given for other rules which the children should decide for themselves, as this will involve them in the valuable process of decision-making. The main coaching points are listed, but these are by no means exhaustive. The teacher will choose those he needs and will include others which are useful for his own particular class. The same principle applies to variations.

Teachers have quite different ideas of basic concepts in games and how they should be taught. Some games are easy enough to understand but the techniques involved require considerable control—for example, rounders and volley-ball, where the techniques or skills need much practice in the initial stages. In other games, such as netball and basketball, the traditional differences between them mask their basic similarities, or at least when they are first introduced.

It is impossible to say at which stage a particular class should start. If a teacher feels his children thoroughly understand a stage then they are probably ready for the next. He may conclude his unit of work with a small tournament or prefer to start a fresh unit with another game to widen his children's experience rather than go on to the next stage of the same game; so much depends on his judgement and facilities.

Generally no sizes of playing areas have been given as these depend on playgrounds, fields and the ability of the children. If a field, pitch or court is marked out, the teacher can organize games 'across' this area and also make good use of the space surrounding it. If necessary he can use lines or skittles or baskets to show real or imaginary boundaries. Children soon learn to recognize their 'own' area.

Diagrams illustrating the various progressions of the following lead-up games can be found at the end of each section on a particular game. 'Equipment' lists include apparatus needed for skill practices.

Progressions of netball and basket-ball games

The following skills have been dealt with on the pages listed.

	Stage 1	Stage 2
throwing and catching	pp. 54–5, 57	pp. 64–5, 66
bouncing and catching	p. 55	pp. 67–8
dribbling	p. 57	p. 65
aiming	pp. 57, 66–8	p. 67–8
dodging and marking	pp. 145–7	pp. 147–9
passing		p. 65

Stages 1 and 2 will be found useful at any age as introductory activities for warming up or to coach particular skills. They should be quite familiar to the children before proceeding further.

Progression of netball and basket-ball   Stage 3
Name of game   2 v. 1

Equipment	One netball or football size 3 or 4 between three players.
Play	Two players are passing to each other, moving about; a third player is trying to intercept the ball.
Rules made by the teacher	1. No contact. 2. No running with the ball (informal—i.e. not strictly enforced).
Rules to be made by the children	1. How do you change over? 2. How do you score? 3. What should be the penalty for breaking the 'no contact' rule?
Coaching	*Catcher* 1. Look for a space to run into to catch the ball. 2. Indicate to your partner where you wish to catch the ball. 3. Watch his eyes and hands for quick catching. 4. Outwit your interceptor by using different dodges. *Thrower* 1. Look for your partner's signs indicating where he wants you to send the ball. 2. Try different kinds of passes. 3. Stand still while you hold the ball; move at once into a new space after you have passed.

Interceptor
1. Make up your mind which of your two opponents you want to mark; then stick to him closely.
2. Remember the 'no contact' rule.
3. See if you can spot your opponent's secret signs.

Variations
1. Use small balls, beanbags or quoits.
2. Tower-ball: two players co-operate trying to knock down the skittle guarded by the third player.

Progression of netball and basket-ball   Stage **4**
Name of game   **2** v. **2**

Equipment
One netball or football size 4 between four players; two braids.

Play
Two players are passing to each other, while their opponents try to intercept the ball.

Rules made by the teacher
1. No contact.
2. No running with the ball (informal).

Rules to be made by the children
1. Decide which couple starts the game.
2. How do you score?
3. Make up your minds who is your own opponent.
4. What should be the penalty for breaking the 'no contact' rule?
5. What should happen if two children catch the ball at the same time?

Coaching
1. Help children, if necessary, to make rules (3) and (4).
2. Coach the 'no running' rule.
3. Encourage a variety of passes.
4. Encourage a variety of dodges.
5. Remind the children to change to attack or defence as the ball changes hands.

Variations
1. Lead-ups to basket-ball:
   a. Allow some dribbling and show how either hand can be used.
   b. Demonstrate shielding the ball by interpolating the body between the opponent and the ball.
   NOTE: too much dribbling is fatal to a fluid game.
2. Use small balls, beanbags or quoits.

3. Limit passes to those that require special practice.
4. Make an area limitation.
5. If there is an odd number of children play 3 v. 2.

Progression of netball and basket-ball

Name of game   **team passing   3** v. **3**

Equipment	One netball or football size 4 between six players; three braids or bibs.
Play	The members of one team pass to each other, while the other team tries to intercept.

Rules made by the teacher
1. No contact.
2. No running with the ball (informal).
3. Area limitation whether formal (lines) or informal.
4. Dribbling is either allowed or not allowed.

Rules to be made by the children
1. Decide which side starts the game.
2. How do you score? Remember that all three team members should participate in the game.
3. Make up your minds who is your own opponent.
4. Make penalties for breaking rules.
5. Choose a captain on each side to make decisions.

Coaching
1. Look at both your team-mates and decide who is in a better position and more likely to catch the ball.
2. Use both your partners.
3. Use a variety of passes and dodges.
4. Use all the available space.
5. If a formal area limitation is made, a throw-in is needed by the opposite side to the one that last touched the ball.

Variations
1. If there are only five children in a group: one child is the thrower, the others are in pairs—for example, two blues and two reds, each child marking one of the other pair. The thrower may pass to the blues who score if they catch the ball; the reds score if they intercept. The ball is returned to the thrower unopposed.

   This is an excellent skill practice at a later stage, simulating the situations listed overleaf:

a. Throw-in from side-line—basket-ball and net-ball;

b. Throw-in by a centre player into the circle—netball;

c. start of game (leaving out opposing centre)—netball.

NOTE: rules are needed for scoring and changing over.

2. If there is an odd number of children, play 4 v. 3.
3. Use small balls, beanbags, quoits or basket-balls.
4. Limit the types of passes allowed.
5. Restrict the area for more skilled players.
6. Use children as umpires.

Progression of netball and basket-ball   Stage **6**
Name of game   **4** v. **4**

Equipment

One netball or football size 4 or 5 between eight players; four braids or bibs; two hoops or chalk circles.

Play

One designated player in each team may stand in his team's hoop or circle. The rest of his team try to throw the ball to him. A goal is scored if he catches the ball while standing in the hoop or circle.

Rules made by the teacher

1. *Either:* both feet must be wholly in the hoop or circle for scoring;

    or: one foot must be inside the hoop, one foot outside.

2. No contact.
3. No running with the ball (informal).
4. Dribbling is either allowed or not allowed.
5. Three passes must be made before scoring may be attempted.
6. The game is restarted by a throw from the opposing team beside the hoop or circle.

Rules to be made by the children

1. Choose a captain on each side to make decisions.
2. Who should start the game?
3. Who should start in the hoop and how do you want to change over? Remember, every player should take his turn.

4. Make penalties for breaking rules.

Coaching

1. *Either:* indicate players' positions at the start of the game;

    or: let children experiment with different positions

2. Encourage quick passing, using a variety of passes.
3. Insist on short passes, no wild flings.
4. Tell children to use all the space, up and down the court and round the hoop or circle.

Variations

1. The goal-catcher can stand on a box or a mat.
2. In a 'difficult' playground the goal-catcher can stand with his back to a wall (but not a low fence).
3. Play a tournament: for example, 3 minutes each way.
4. Use children as umpires.
5. An area limitation can be made, which involves throwing-in if the ball crosses the line.
6. Use small balls, beanbags or quoits.

Progression of netball and basket-ball   Stage **7**
Name of game   **5** v. **5**

Equipment

One netball or football between ten players; five braids or bibs; two targets: hoops, chalk lines or playground mats.

Play

Each team tries to *bounce* the ball in their opponent's hoop or chalk figure or on their mats. A goal is scored if the ball is bounced, not rolled in the hoop, figure or on the mat.

Rules made by by the teacher

1. Dribbling is either allowed or not allowed.
2. No contact.
3. No running with the ball (informal).
4. The game is restarted after a goal by a throw by the opposing team beside the target.
5. Have a centre-line if necessary (see variation 1).

Rules to be made by the children

1. Choose captains.
2. Do you need a goalkeeper?
3. Decide on every player's position and opponent at the start of the game.

4. Make penalties for breaking rules.

Coaching	1. Use all the space, keeping well away from each other. (If all the children converge on the target add a centre-line; see variation 1.) 2. Change swiftly from attack to defence, move ahead of the ball into a position for shooting. 3. Try using short passes. (If the children find this difficult, indicate a number of passes—for example, four—before a shot at goal may be attempted.)
Variations	1. Draw a centre-line; only the centres may pass it. This divides the players into attacks and defences, reduces the crowding round the target and assures several passes before a goal is attempted. It tends to slow down the game. An off-side rule is needed. 2. Impose an area limitation involving a throwing-in rule. 3. Add a special area for a goalkeeper. 4. Use an umpire for decision-making.

Progression of netball and basket-ball   Stage **8**
Name of game   **skittle-ball   6** v. **6**

Equipment	One netball or football between twelve players; six braids or bibs, two skittles; playground chalk.
Play	Each team tries to knock down their opponents' skittle. Only the goalkeeper may enter the circle, and a goal is scored even if he knocks down his own skittle.
Rules made by the teacher	1. Dribbling is either allowed or not allowed. 2. The goalkeeper may—or may not—be allowed to come out of his area. 3. The game is restarted by a throw-up between the centres *or* by alternate centre passes. 4. No contact, no running with the ball (informal), off-side, two-on-the-ball rules.
Rules to be made by the children	1. Choose captains. 2. Agree on starting positions, opposing pairs of

players, changing over the goalkeepers, changing ends and penalties.

3. Should the goalkeeper be allowed to catch the ball?

Coaching

1. Move ahead of the ball and round the circle to shoot.
2. Do not crowd round the circle but distribute yourselves round the edge of it.
3. The rules decided on must be strictly kept.
4. Concentrate on swift changes from defence to attack and vice versa.

Variations

1. Apply netball or basket-ball footwork rules as follows: the player holding or catching the ball may pivot and land on one foot and step on the other in any direction; land on two feet and step on one in any direction; a jump may follow either, but the ball must leave the player's hands before either foot touches the ground again.
2. Area limitations (see Stage 9).
3. If there is a severe shortage of apparatus, a quoit can be used instead of a ball.
4. Play 5-a-side, with a designated goalkeeper or centre.
5. Use an umpire for decision-making.

Progression of netball and basket-ball   Stage **9**
Name of game   **two-court netball 6** v. **6**

Equipment

One netball or football beween twelve players; six braids or bibs; playground chalk; two netball posts.

Play

Each team tries to shoot goals from *outside* the circle, but inside the court; only one goalkeeper is allowed inside the circle.

Rules made by the teacher

1. Shots may be attempted from anywhere outside the circle, and inside the court.
2. If the ball goes outside the boundaries it is thrown in by a member of the opposite team at the point where it crossed the line.
3. All other rules as for Stage 8.

Rules to be made *by the children*	1. As for Stage 8. 2. Should the goalkeeper be allowed to throw in? 3. Should the off-side rule be applied to throw-ins? 4. Agree on penalties for breaking rules.
Coaching	1. Tell *any* child in a suitable position to shoot. 2. Allow any kind of shot but demonstrate and encourage the two-handed shot, one hand supplying the force, the other the direction. 3. Encourage jump shots, the arms stretching in mid-air (see Stage 10). 4. Teach the children to aim slightly above the rim of the basket, eyes focused on the target.
Variation	Use an umpire, not the captains, to make decisions.

Progression of netball and basket-ball   Stage **10**
Name of game   **skittle basket-ball**   **5** v. **5**

Equipment	One basket-ball; five braids or bibs; two skittles; playground chalk.
Play	Using basket-ball rules, each team tries to knock down their opponent's skittle.
Rules made by *the teacher*	1. Start with a jump ball between the centres. 2. Only the goalkeeper is allowed in the circle. 3. Close marking is allowed but no personal contact. 4. After a goal, the game is restarted by the defending side from a point near the circle.
Rules to be made *by the children*	1. Decide on ends, captains and positions of players; choose goalkeepers. 2. Should other players beside the goalkeeper be allowed to cross the circle? 3. Organize a system of defence around your circle.
Coaching	1. After a goal, the game should be restarted quickly; children designated as defence must immediately run to their positions near their own circle. 2. Discourage too much dribbling. 3. Encourage fast passing and shooting from all directions, using all members of the team.

Variations

1. Use a netball post as in Stage 9. This involves jump shots.
   (NOTE: hold the ball directly in front of the nose. Jump in the air, stretch arms and release the ball at the highest point. Two hands give both force and balance.)
2. Use a ring and basket-ball backboard against a wall at one end; the other goal could be free-standing as above.

For Stage 11, junior netball, see rules published by the All England Netball Association.

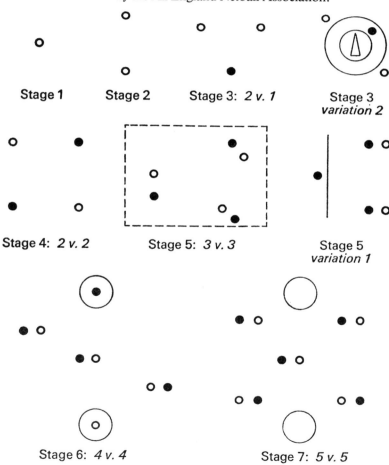

Stage 1

Stage 2

Stage 3: *2 v. 1*

Stage 3
variation 2

Stage 4: *2 v. 2*

Stage 5: *3 v. 3*

Stage 5
variation 1

Stage 6: *4 v. 4*

Stage 7: *5 v. 5*

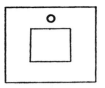

Playground mat with chalk line

Hoop with chalk circle

Chalk lines

Stage 7: *variation 3*

Stage 8: *6 v. 6*

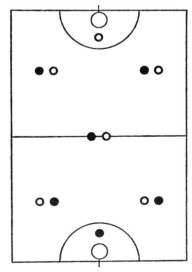

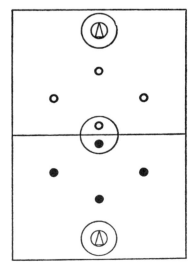

Stage 9: *6 v. 6*

Stage 10
skittle basket-ball, 4 v. 4, 5 v. 5

Shinty and hockey

Progression of shinty and hockey — Stage **1**
Name of game   **1** v. **1**

Equipment

One shinty, unihoc, polypropylene or junior hockey stick and one shinty or composition hockey ball per child.

Play

Try to hit the ball over your opponent's base-line—this scores one goal. Start the game with a push back from the centre-line.

Basic rules made by the teacher

1. Wait for the push back before the game actually begins.
2. The stick must not be lifted above shoulder level.
3. Do not hit—even unintentionally—your opponent's stick or leg.
4. Use the flat side of the hockey stick.

Rules to be made by the children

1. Which end do you want to aim at?
2. What should be the penalty for breaking the teacher's rules?

Coaching

1. Dribbling: keep the ball close to the stick.
2. 'Sticks' rule: the stick must not be lifted above shoulder level at *any time*.
3. Keep in *control* of the ball; do not hit wildly.
4. Restart the game repeatedly from the centre-line. (If discipline is good, each couple should continue without waiting for the other children.)

Progression of shinty and hockey — Stage **2**
Name of game   **2** v. **2**

Equipment

A shinty, unihoc, polypropylene or hockey stick per child; one ball between two; two braids or bibs.

Play

Each team tries to hit the ball across their opponents' base-line. Start with a push back from the centre-line.

Rules made by the teacher

1. Basic rules as for Stage 1.
2. Two (or more) passes must be made before hitting the ball over the base-line.
3. The side against which the goal has just been scored restarts with a push back.

Rules to be made by the children	1. Who starts the game? 2. How do you change over? 3. Agree on penalties
Coaching	1. Passing: demonstrate the two different grips: hands *slightly* apart and body facing forward for dribbling and pushing, hands together and sideways stance for hitting; correct any awkward hold. The hands should be on opposite sides of the stick. Let children experiment with hitting and stopping; encourage them to move about. 2. In the game emphasize co-operation between partners.
Variation	3 v. 3. For tackling and intercepting see Stage 3.

Progression of shinty and hockey   Stage **3**
Name of game   **4** v. **4**

Equipment	One shinty, unihoc, polypropylene or hockey stick per child; one ball between two; four braids or bibs.
Play	Teams: three attacks, one defence. Try to hit the ball over your opponents' base-line. If the defence hits the ball over the base-line, a corner is taken by the attacking team.
Rules made by the teacher	1. Basic rules as for Stage 1 and 2. 2. Make four passes before attempting to score. 3. Face your opponent when you tackle (basic rule).
Rules to be made by the children	1. Who plays in each position? Who is the captain? 2. Organize a system of changing positions. 3. Is the defending player allowed to shoot goals? 4. Agree on penalties.
Coaching	1. General: co-operation between members of each team in attack and defence. 2. Skill practices. Intercepting: two players pass the ball to each other, moving in one direction. They try to outwit their opponent by passing in front or behind him. The interceptor watches the child with the ball, and guards the space between the two players. 3. Dodging and tackling: two players face each other

some distance apart, the child with the ball trying to dodge past his opponent, keeping control of the ball. Each must remember to keep facing his opponent and not infringe the basic rules.

4. The children choose an umpire (to use a whistle).

Variation 5 v. 5. Skill practice: 3 v. 2.

Progression of shinty and hockey Stage **4**
Name of game **6** v. **6**

Equipment One shinty, unihoc, polypropylene or hockey stick per child; one ball between twelve; practice balls; six braids or bibs; goal-posts: four stumps or skittles.

Play Teams: three attacks and three defences.
Try to score goals by hitting the ball between your opponents' goal-posts. If the ball goes over the base-line outside the goal-posts, restart the game with a corner, or hit-out if the offender is an attacker.

Rules made by the teacher
1. Basic rules as for Stage 3.
2. Side-lines may be needed at this stage: push or hit by the opposite side to the player who last touched it, from the place where the ball crossed the line.
3. Goals: a hit knocking over a goal-post is *not* scored as a goal.

Rules to be made by the children
1. Who plays in each position? Who is the captain?
2. Are the defending players allowed to score goals?
3. Agree on penalties.

Coaching
1. The defences and attacks should co-operate. The defences must be alert to back each other up.
2. Keep the game 'fluid' but make children aware of different functions of attacks and defences.
3. Keep the game spread out. Encourage passes from one side to the other.
4. Shooting: practise this individually, from a pass and against opposition; aim at control and accuracy. Spend as little time as possible on stationary work: controlling the ball and turning to shoot from a pass is far more useful. Use skill practices described at Stage 3.

5. Practise passing, intercepting and shooting, 3 v. 2.
6. The children should choose an umpire.
7. Hit-out taken by a defender opposite where the ball went off, level with the front edge of the shooting circle, or an appropriate distance from base-line.

Progression of shinty and hockey   Stage 5
Name of game   6 v. 6

Equipment

Shinty, unihoc, polypropylene or hockey stick per child, one ball between twelve, practice balls, six braids or bibs, goal-posts.

Play

Teams: three attacks and three defences, one of whom is designated as goalkeeper. Try to score goals from inside the circle by hitting the ball between the goal-posts. If the ball goes over the base-line from an attacker's stick, a hit-out is taken from the circle edge; if from a defence's stick, a corner hit must be taken.

Rules made by the teacher

1. All previous rules.
2. Corner hits: if a defender hits the ball over the base-line, a corner hit is taken by a member of the attacking team; all other attacks stand outside the circle, defences behind the base-line.
3. Penalties for all other fouls: a free hit to the opposing team.

Rules to be made by the children

1. Who plays in each position. Who is the captain? Who is the goalkeeper? Who is the umpire?
2. Who should take free hits, side-line hits, corner hits and hit-outs?
3. Should the goalkeeper have any special privileges?

Coaching

1. Group practices for corner hits: defences behind the base-line, attacks outside the circle.
2. Pay attention to the distribution of the game. The centre and goalkeeper, in particular, need to pass to both sides of the pitch.
3. Both fluidity and division of function is important. Each child should be alert to back up his team.

Variation

Play a 6-a-side tournament. Let the children choose whether to designate a goalkeeper or not.

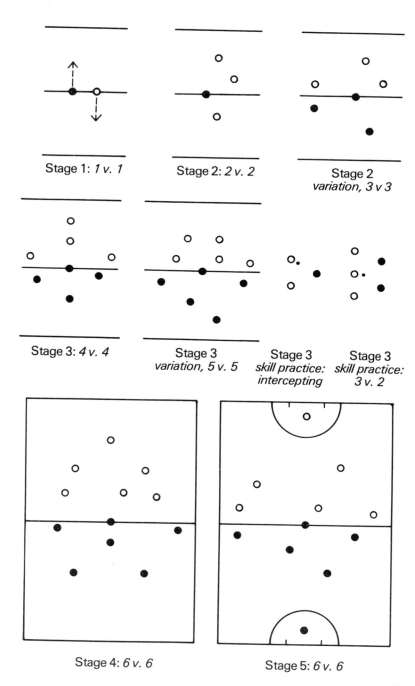

Stage 1: *1 v. 1*

Stage 2: *2 v. 2*

Stage 2
variation, 3 v 3

Stage 3: *4 v. 4*

Stage 3
variation, 5 v. 5

Stage 3
*skill practice:
intercepting*

Stage 3
*skill practice:
3 v. 2*

Stage 4: *6 v. 6*

Stage 5: *6 v. 6*

Football

Progression of football Stage **1**

Name of game **individual play**

Equipment   One ball per child, made of strong, moulded plastic.

Skills   Dribbling, kicking, using all sides of both feet; volleying, heading.

'Beat your own record activities:

Type 1

Find all the different parts of your feet you can use for kicking the ball.

Type 2

a. How fast can you dribble your ball without losing it.

b. How long can you go on dribbling your ball without losing it?

c. Dribble and kick your ball so that it rises—or does not rise—from the ground.

d. Throw your ball in the air and head it with your forehead. Keep your eyes on your ball.

Progression of football Stage **2**

Name of game **1** v. **1**

Equipment   One ball between two players; any open space with base-lines marked; preferably also a centre-line.

Play   Dribble and kick your ball over your opponent's base-line.

Rules made by the teacher   1. Do not kick or bump into your opponent.

Rules to be made by the children   1. Who starts the game?
2. Who should re-start the game after a goal?

Coaching   *Skills in preparation for succeeding games:*
Co-operating in pairs
1. Dribble and kick the ball in pairs; kick ahead of your partner, kick with either foot.
2. Kick high, your partner trapping the ball with parts of his body.
No handling.
3. Throw and head or volley and head the ball.

Opposing each other
1. Tackling and feinting: no. 1 with the ball, no. 2

facing some distance away. No. 1 try to pass no. 2 by feinting and shielding the ball. Use twists and turns and changes in speed. No. 2 observe your opponent and tackle unexpectedly.

2. No. 2 tackle from behind; remember not to touch your opponent.

Progression of football
Name of game **2** v. **2**
Stage **3**

Equipment	One ball between three players; two braids or bibs; base-lines and centre-line.
Play	Kick your ball over your opponents' base-line.

Rules made by the teacher
1. Do not kick or bump into your opponents.
2. Make at least two passes before kicking for a goal.
3. The side against which the goal has just been scored kicks off.

Rules to be made by the children
1. Which side starts the game?
2. When do you change the player kicking off?

Co-operating in attack and defence
1. 2 v. 1. Two players passing: use different passes, disguise your passes. One player tackling; anticipate every move; keep between your opponents, move backwards if necessary; do not be drawn to tackle one or the other, but *intercept* the ball as it crosses the space between your opponents.
2. 1 v. 2. A single player tries to pass two opponents one after the other;
(NOTE: the two opponents must *not* tackle at the same time. Encourage close dribbling, twisting and turning to shield the ball. Children should make the rules.)

Progression of football
Name of game **3** v. **3**
Stage **4**

Equipment	One ball between two players; three braids or bibs; base-lines and centre-line.

Play	Kick your ball over your opponents' base-line.
Rules made by the teacher	1. Do not kick or bump into your opponents. 2. Make at least three passes before kicking for a goal. 3. The side against which a goal is scored kicks off.
Rules to be made by the children	1. On which side of the centre should the second forward stand? 2. Should the defender be allowed to shoot? If so, should another player temporarily change over? 3. Devise a scheme for changing round all the positions.
Coaching	*Skill practices* 1. Pass in twos and threes, using both feet. Pass to alternate sides. 2. Use different parts of the body to trap the ball. 3. Combine these practices with two players kicking the ball towards a third who must trap it and immediately pass it to the opposite side. 4. Play intercepting in threes, using all the skills you have learnt so far. *Game* Co-operation between three players. Preserve 'fluidity', that is, as differentiation of function becomes important, show how players can interchange.

Progression of football   Stage **5**
Name of game   **4** v. **4**

Equipment	One ball between two players; four braids or bibs; goal-lines and centre-line; goal-posts (stumps).
Play	Play a game of 4-a-side. Score one goal every time you kick the ball between your opponents' goal-posts.
Rules made by the teacher	1. Make at least four passes before kicking for goal between the goal-posts. 2. Kick off as before; no personal contact as before. 3. If the ball goes over the base-line from an attacker, the defender takes a free kick from just outside the goal. Only indirect kicks at the goal are then allowed.

4. If the ball goes over the base-line from the defender, an attacker has a corner kick from a specified point. Direct kicks at goal from a corner kick are allowed.

Rules to be made by the children

1. Who should start the game?
2. Decide on a scheme for changing over positions.
3. Should the defender be allowed to shoot?
4. Should the defender be allowed to handle the ball?
5. Which attacker takes a corner?

Coaching

Skill practices
1. Defenders practise long kicks forward in pairs.
2. 2 v. 1. Trap the ball from a pass and shoot against a defender.
3. 3 v. 1. Pass and shoot in threes against a defender.
4. Kick from the corner (that is, a stationary ball). Decide if the defender should have special powers of handling the ball and act as goalkeeper. (This will probably require special practice and may or may not be suitable on a particular field.)

Game
The defender should keep between the attackers and the goal. Attackers should run back and help in defence as required. Both 'fluidity' and good positioning are vital. An indirect kick means that a shot at goal may not be attempted by the player taking the kick; it must be touched by another player first. A direct kick means a goal kick may be attempted after the corner kick has been taken.

Progression of football   Stage **6**
Name of game   **5** v. **5**

Equipment

One ball between two players; five braids or bibs; goal-lines, side-lines, centre-line, goal-posts; a slightly longer field if possible.

Play

Play a game of 5-a-side.

Rules made by the teacher

1. No passing restrictions before shooting; the ball may be kicked high.
2. No personal contact.

3. A corner kick if the ball goes over the base-line from a defender. One of the defenders has a free kick from goal if an attacker sends the ball off.
4. A member of the opposite team throws in from the spot where the ball crossed the side-line.

Rules to be made by the children
1. Should one of the defenders be designated as goalkeeper?
2. Choose a captain for each side to make decisions —unless you have a referee. If the captains cannot agree, the teacher is still the final arbiter.
3. Change the referee from time to time.

Coaching
Skill practices
1. Practise throw-ins, lob passes, dips and volleys. Play 2 v. 1 for throw-ins.
2. Play intercepting in threes, coaching these passes.
3. Play attackers against defenders, that is, 3 v. 2. Coach co-operation and variety of passing and feinting.

Game
1. Coach interchanging of players while keeping the game spread out; *no* interchanging otherwise.
2. Coach use of throw-ins.
3. A player may, but need not be, designated as goalkeeper. It is better to allow lots of goals; but as the game gets more accurate, a goalkeeper may be unavoidable. Discuss this with the children.
4. Coach passing up the field and encourage plenty of clearing passes. Use the centre-forward as a pivot distributing the game from side to side.
5. Have a referee with a whistle and let him make decisions. Change the referee frequently. If the children quarrel, discuss the rules.

Progression of football   Stage **7**
Name of game   **6** v. **6**

Equipment
One ball between players; six braids or bibs; field marked with centre circle, goal- and side-lines; goal-posts and line indicating goal area.

Play
Play a game of 6-a-side.

Rules made by the teacher	1. The goalkeeper may punch, handle and dive on the ball in his goal area. 2. Goals may be kicked from anywhere on the field.
Rules to be made by the children	1. Choose captains and organize your teams. 2. Designate goalkeepers. 3. Choose ends and who should kick off. 4. Choose a referee. 5. Remember that the teams must change ends.
Coaching	*Skill practices* 1. Goal-keeping—coach jumping in all directions. Coach two-handed punches. The jump in the air should be made before the arms are extended. 2. Practise diving on the ball and rolling over, in pairs. 3. Practise long clearances in pairs. Play 2 v. 1: two attackers, one goalkeeper. 　　　3 v. 1: three attackers, one goalkeeper. 　　　3 v. 2: three attackers, one goalkeeper and one defender. 　　　3 v. 3: three attackers and three defenders.

Game
1. Coach co-operation within the team.
2. Allow interchanging as long as the game keeps spread out.
3. Make further rules as necessary.

Stage 1 *individual play*　　　Stage 2: *1 v. 1*

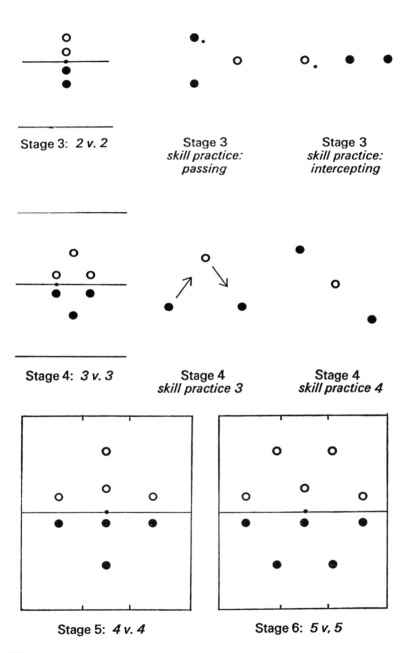

Stage 3: *2 v. 2*

Stage 3
*skill practice:
passing*

Stage 3
*skill practice:
intercepting*

Stage 4: *3 v. 3*

Stage 4
skill practice 3

Stage 4
skill practice 4

Stage 5: *4 v. 4*

Stage 6: *5 v, 5*

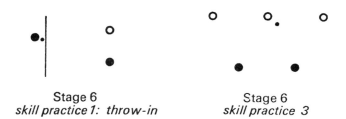

Stage 6
skill practice 1: throw-in

Stage 6
skill practice 3

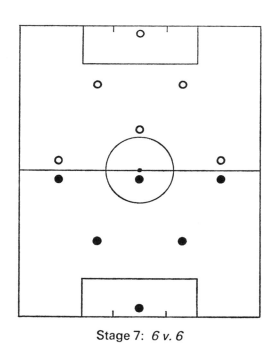

Stage 7: *6 v. 6*

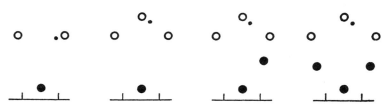

Stage 7 *skill practices 3: shooting and goalkeeping*

Padder-tennis

Progression of padder-tennis   Stage **1**
     Name of game   **individual play**

Equipment   One bat and ball per child.

Play   Individual play with bat and ball. Both air-flow and
                     rubber balls are useful.
                     Experiments should lead to volleying, bouncing and
                     hitting.

Progression of padder-tennis   Stage **2**
     Name of game   **passing in pairs**

Equipment   One bat per child; one ball between two—either
                     rubber or tennis core.

Play   Passing in pairs: hit both high and low on either side
                     of you, either letting the ball bounce once or twice
                     or volleying it.
                     Aiming in pairs: adjust to each other's play.

Coaching   1. Stand far enough apart to be able to hit force-
                        fully.
                     2. Turn your whole body to hit from *both* sides of
                        you.
                     3. Swing the arm you use for hitting.

Progression of padder-tennis   Stage **3**
     Name of game   **passing over a net**

Equipment   One playbat or padder-tennis bat per child; one ball
                     between two; posts, nets or ropes.
                     (See also pp. 68–73).

Play   Make up a game of hitting across the net.

Rules made by   1. *Either:* use playbats or air-flow balls;
the teacher   *or:* use padder-tennis or *strong* playbats with
                               rubber or tennis balls.
                     2. Set a 'Beat your own record' activity.

Rules to be made	1. Who starts the game?
by the children	2. How do you score?
	3. Is the ball allowed to bounce?
	4. Is it harder to hit the ball from one side of your body than the other? Count two points for every hit from the harder side.
Coaching	*Lightweight bats*
	1. Face the net; keep your wrists supple.
	2. Stand fairly close to the net, but do not touch it.
	3. Watch your opponent's bat and ball.
	4. Vary the height, strength and speed of your hit.
	Strong bats
	1. Stand well back from the net; let the ball bounce and hit it on the rise. Keep your wrist firm.
	2. Hit from *either side of you.* Practise the change of grip.
	(NOTE: insist on this with older juniors.)
	3. Experiment with keeping the ball low.
	4. Experiment with different heights, lengths and speeds of hits.
	5. Experiment with different services.
	6. Keep on your toes, ready to move in all directions.

Progression of padder-tennis
Name of game 2 v. 2
Stage 4

Equipment	Playbat or padder-tennis bat per child; one ball between four; posts with nets or ropes 3 metres–6 metres across.
Play	Make up a game of hitting across the net.
Rules made by the teacher	1. Decide on equipment.
	2. No individual scores: each side scores together.
Rules to be made by the children	1. Who starts the game and how?
	2. How do you score?
	3. Is the ball allowed to bounce once or twice?
	4. Who takes the ball if it bounces between you?
Coaching	*General*
	1. Co-operate with your partner.
	2. Be ready to move while you watch the ball.

3. Look at the spot you want to aim at, *before* your bat makes contact with the ball.
4. Be aware of where your partner is all the time.

Lightweight bats
1. Avoid hitting balls high, which gives your opponents the opportunity to smash.
2. Smash whenever you can.
3. Try to hit into a *space*: for example, between your opponents or out to the side.

Strong bats
1. Use correct forehand and backhand grips, turn your body sideways to the net and swing your whole arm.
2. Experiment with different hits.
3. Look at your opponent's bat and see if you can guess where his ball will bounce.

Progression of padder-tennis

Stage **5**

Name of game **2** v. **2**

(with base- and side-lines)

Equipment	Four padder-tennis bats, four balls, posts and nets or ropes, playground chalk; court: 6 × 13 metres; allow space round each court.
Play	Make up a game over the net, using over-arm or under-arm service.
Rules made by the teacher	1. A ball touching a line is 'in'. 2. A ball touching the net during a service is a 'let' and must be repeated; ignore 'lets' during the game. 3. Receiver: the service must bounce once before you can hit it.
Rules to be made by the children	1. Decide on the order of service. Who starts? 2. How do you score? Who should call the score? 3. During the game, should the ball bounce more than once?
Coaching	1. Use forehand and backhand grips for drives and volleys. 2. Drives: start your swing in good time, using the

whole arm—do not tuck your elbow in; hit hard.

3. Stand well back (that is, within 1 metre of the base-line), so that you can play 'good-length' strokes.

4. Volleys: hold bat firmly in forehand or backhand grips; punch really hard; experiment with direction.

5. Over-arm service: stand sideways to the net, behind the base-line. Change your weight from the front to the back foot and screw your whole body backward and upward, swinging your bat high; at the same time throw your ball in the air as high as you can reach, 30 cm to the right and in front of you; then come down really hard on the ball. Practise hitting all four balls one after the other, then change over with your partner.

Under-arm service: bounce your ball or throw it up, then hit it like a forehand drive. Always look first at the spot you are aiming at before you hit, then concentrate on the ball all the time.

Progression of padder-tennis   Stage **6**
Name of game   **padder-tennis**

Equipment   Four padder-tennis bats and four to six balls; posts with nets or ropes; playground-chalk lines or permanent markings. Allow space round each court; for dimensions see Stage 5.

Play   Scorer starts serving from right-hand court into the diagonally opposite court; receiver must allow the ball to bounce once before it is in play. Score as in tennis: love, 15, 30, 40, game; or deuce, advantage server or receiver, game. The server continues serving for a whole game.

Rules made by by the teacher
1. Any special rules regarding space.
2. The server must have two balls ready before he serves.
3. The server's partner is responsible for fielding the balls and supplying his partner.
4. The umpire's decision is final.

Rules to be made
by the children

1. Are under-arm services allowed?
2. Who starts serving on each side?
3. How often should you change ends, especially on a sunny day?
4. Who should call the score after each point?

Coaching

1. Teach the positioning for all four players, especially the server and receiver.
2. Observation and anticipation of hits: encourage children to think in terms of 'possible angles of return' and to move half-way between.
3. Encourage movement about the court.
4. Encourage deliberate placing of every hit.
5. If umpires are available let them call out the score; remind children that the umpire's decision must be accepted and that he sometimes sees things the players cannot see.

Stage 1 *individual play*   Stage 2 *passing in pairs*

Stage 3 *passing over a net*   Stage 4: *2 v. 2*

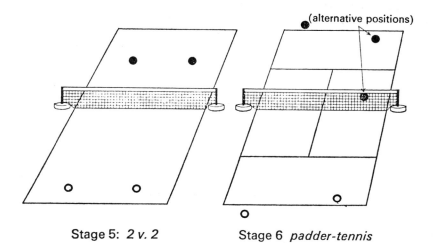

Stage 5: *2 v. 2*   Stage 6 *padder-tennis*

Quoit- or deck-tennis

Progression of quoit- or deck-tennis   Stage 1, 2, 3A

Stage 1: see p. 61 and diagram on p. 113.
Stage 2: see pp. 64, 66 and diagram on p. 113.
Stage 3A: see pp. 71, 72.

Progression of quoit- or deck-tennis   Stage 3B
Name of game   1 v. 1

Equipment	One quoit between two children; posts and nets or ropes at children's shoulder-height.
Play	Make up a game of throwing and catching—for example, *either:* each player starts the game five times; *or:* take it in turns to start the game.

Rules made by the teacher

1. The quoit must be thrown horizontally without wobbling.
2. The quoit must be thrown with the same hand that caught it.
3. The quoit may be caught with either hand but must not touch the body.
4. Scoring: count the number of times your opponent *fails* to catch or uses two hands or his body.
5. Change ends after each game.

Rules to be made by the children

1. Who starts the game?
2. How many points make up a game?
3. If the quoit touches the net, should you repeat the throw or let it pass?

Coaching

1. Play is different from Stage 3A, p. 72, and needs explaining:
   Look for a space where your opponent finds it difficult to catch. Count a point for yourself every time your opponent drops the quoit or uses two hands or his body.
2. Throw at once from the spot where you caught the quoit.
3. Look at your opponent's eyes and hand and think where he will throw the quoit.

Progression of quoit- or deck-tennis
Name of game   **2** v. **2**

Equipment	One quoit between four children; posts and nets or ropes.
Play	Make up a game of throwing and catching. Take it in turns to serve. Only correct throws and catches count.
Rules made by the teacher	1. The quoit must be thrown horizontally without wobbling.
	2. The quoit may be caught with either hand and thrown with the same hand.
	3. Scoring: only the serving side scores, as in Stage 3B.
	4. Change ends after each game.
Rules to be made by the children	1. Who should start a game? Keep the same order of serving throughout.
	2. How many points make up a game?
	3. If the quoit touches the net, should you repeat the throw or let it pass?
	4. Who should take the catch if the quoit is aimed between you and your partner?
Coaching	1. Co-operation between players on each side: either coach one to stand forward and one back, or both side by side.
	2. Encourage children to keep on their toes and to watch their opponent's eyes and feet.
	3. Remind children of the order of serving—which *they* have decided on.
	4. Have either an umpire or the server call out the score after every point.
Variation	Score a point every time either side *catches* the quoit. This is an easier method of scoring.

Progression of quoit- or deck-tennis
Name of game   **2** v. **2**

(with neutral ground either side of the net and boundary-lines)

Equipment	One quoit between four children; posts, nets or ropes, playground chalk.

Play	A and B play against C and D, A starts serving followed by C, B and D in turn. The server continues serving from alternate sides until his side loses a point. Each player starts serving from the starting-line you will agree on.
Rules made by the teacher	1. Only the serving side can call the score. 2. A point is scored if the quoit is dropped in the receiving side's area. If the quoit touches the neutral ground or boundary-lines it is considered within the area. If it goes outside the boundary-lines, or drops completely in the neutral ground, the serving side loses the point. 3. The quoit must be caught with one hand and thrown with the same hand from the point where it was caught, even if that was outside the lines. 4. Two players may catch the quoit at the same time, provided it has not touched the body of either of them. Either player can throw it. 5. No player may step into the neutral ground.
Rules to be made by the children	1. Who should serve first on each side? 2. How many points make up a game? 3. Decide where you should serve from: for example, behind or just inside the base-line, or farther forward. 4. Can either of you catch the service?
Coaching	1. The order of serving must be A, C, B, D. 2. Stress the rules regarding boundary-lines, neutral ground and 'let'. 3. Explain the teacher's rule 4 by demonstrating it. 4. Either an umpire or the server should call out the score after each point. 5. Play a tournament. All the children involved must agree on rules to be used. 6. Encourage short and long passes, and use of empty spaces.
Variation	Score points to each side as they catch the quoit if catching is poor.

110

Progression of quoit- or deck-tennis   Stage **6**
Name of game   **deck-tennis**

Equipment	One quoit between four children; posts and nets, playground chalk; size of court: 6 × 12 metres or smaller, divided into neutral area and four playing areas.
Play	Service: A starts serving from the right-hand side to his opponent in the diagonally-opposite court and then from alternate sides, always behind the base-lines; he remains in the right-hand court to receive service from C. B will start serving from the left-hand court. C will start serving from the right-hand court and D from the left-hand court, on the other side. Only the serving side can score.
Rules made by the teacher	1. The service is taken from behind the base-line. 2. The service must be received by the opponent in the diagonally-opposite court; after this it is in general play. 3. Rules for quoit handling, boundary-lines, neutral ground and 'let' as before; if the quoit touches the service-court line it is considered 'in'.
Rules to be made by the children	1. Decide on the order of serving and receiving. 2. How many points make up a game?
Coaching	1. Receive in the correct order. 2. Players stand *either* forward and back *or* side by side; if side-by-side play is adopted the players should remain on a level and return to the centre of their own side after every throw and make up their minds who should take doubtful passes. 3. Practise services from behind the base-line to the court diagonally opposite, and from different positions behind that line. 4. Outwit your opponents, using different passes.
Variation	Scoring: supposing the children decided the game should consist of 10 points, when 9-all is reached the best of 3 could decide the winners.

Name of game   **quoit-tennis**

Equipment	One quoit between four children; posts, nets, play-ground chalk; size of court: 6 × 12 metres or smaller.
Play	One player serves for the whole of one game. He serves from the right-hand side to the diagonally-opposite service court and then alternately left and right. Scoring as in tennis; love, 15, 30, 40, game; or deuce, advantage server or receiver and game. Each point is scored either to the serving or receiving side. Quoit handling, service, 'let', and line decisions as previously.
Rules to be made by the children	1. Decide on the order of serving and receiving.
Coaching	1. Order of play and scoring.

1. Order of play and scoring.
2. Point out the differences if Stage 6 has been played previously.
3. Players should normally play on the right- or left-hand side, but crossing over is allowed and can be taken advantage of.
4. Encourage children to experiment with different starting positions.
5. Suggest that children experiment with various positions relative to each other during the game (compare with padder-tennis).
6. Encourage them to use long and short passes and to outwit their opponents.

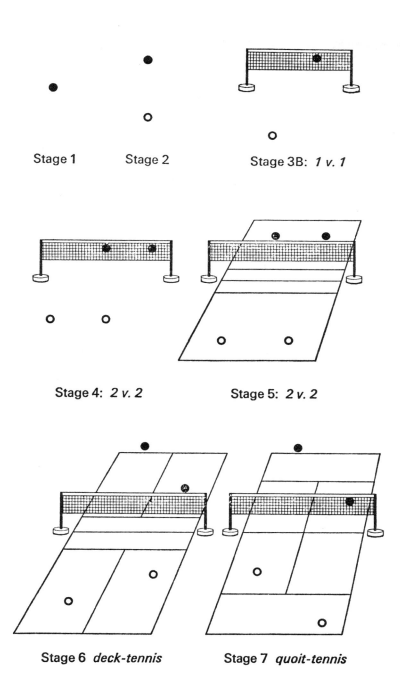

Stage 1 Stage 2 Stage 3B: *1 v. 1*

Stage 4: *2 v. 2* Stage 5: *2 v. 2*

Stage 6 *deck-tennis* Stage 7 *quoit-tennis*

Volley-ball
Progression of volley-ball

Use light-weight plastic balls, size 4.

Let children throw and catch as well as pat and volley the ball.

They should aim at grounding it on the opponent's side, and should realize they can only score by aiming the ball so that it is difficult to catch and return.

Stage 1: practise individually.

Stage 2: practise in pairs.

Stage 3: practise in pairs over a net at reach-height.

Progression of volley-ball

Stage **4**

Name of game:
informal Newcombe 2 v. **2**

Equipment	One light-weight plastic ball between four children; posts with nets or ropes.
Play	Make up a game of throwing and catching over the net, trying to hit the ground on the other side. Take it in turns to serve.
Rules to be made by the teacher	1. The server continues to serve until he loses a point; then the other side starts serving. Keep the same order of serving throughout. 2. One or two hands may be used to catch the ball.
Rules to be made by the children	1. Who should start the game? 2. How many points make up a game?
	1. Co-operate with your partner. You can pass to each other before passing over the net. 2. Practise batting the ball over the net in preparation for succeeding games; bend your wrists backward, and relax your fingers. 3. Practise setting the ball up, your partner batting it over the net or rope. 4. Practise serving, increasing your distance from the net. (See Stage 5, coaching 3.)
Variation	Use boundary-lines. A more formal game results. The server must serve from behind the base-line.

Progression of volley-ball Stage **5**
Name of game **prisoner ball** **3** v. **3**

Equipment	One light-weight plastic ball size 4; posts and nets or ropes.
Play	Volley the ball over the net. On winning a point, the server chooses a prisoner from the other side, who continues playing on the server's side. The game ends when one team has made prisoners of the opposing team.
Rules made by the teacher	1. Only one prisoner may be captured with each point. 2. If the ball touches the net during the service and goes over (called 'let'), the service is repeated. If this happens during the game, play on. 3. The ball may be batted any number of times on the same side, but must not touch the ground.
Rules to be made by the children	1. Decide your order of service. 2. Consider who would be your best prisoner. 3. Draw a line for service on the right-hand side of the playing area.
Coaching	1. Backing up: be alert to help each other. 2. The same child *may* set the ball up and bat it. 3. Service: throw the ball up and hit it with the clenched fist or with the knuckles facing up. The hand and wrist should be firm, not rigid.
Variations	1. Use boundary-lines. A more formal game results. The court should not be too long or wide. 2. Play the game with Newcombe rules, i.e. the ball may be caught and thrown. 3. Allow the ball to be batted three times only on any one side, before crossing the net. 4. Play 4 v. 4.

Progression of volley-ball Stage **6**
Name of game **4** v. **4**

Equipment	One light-weight plastic ball, size 4; posts with nets or ropes, playground chalk or permanent markings. The pitch should not be too big.

Play	Volley the ball over the net. A point is scored by the serving side if they succeed in grounding the ball within their opponents' court or if it goes off an opponent out of court. If the point is lost by the serving side, the opposing side starts serving.
Rules made by the teacher	1. Each team-member changes round one place in a clockwise direction, whenever it is their side's turn to serve. The service is taken behind the back-line in the service area. 2. The ball must be batted with one or both hands—not thrown, and must be volleyed—not caught. 3. It may be played any number of times on the same side of the net.
Rules to be made by the children	1. Which side starts serving? 2. What are the players' starting positions? 3. How many points make a game?
Coaching	1. Practise serving from the correct service area; other players can help it over the net. 2. Practise change-over *before* a new server starts. 3. Practise setting up and batting. 4. Work together as a team; watch your opponents' handling of the ball and think where it is likely to drop; avoid crowding.
Variation	Play 5 v. 5.

Progression of volley-ball   Stage 7
Name of game   6 v. 6

Equipment	One light-weight plastic ball or volley-ball; posts with nets or ropes; chalk or permanent markings.
Play	Volley the ball over the net. Score by grounding the ball on the opposite side.
Rules made by the teacher	1. Number the members of your team and change round one place at each change of service. 2. Each player may only bat the ball once, but may do so again if another player has touched it in between. 3. The ball may be played any number of times on the same side.

| *Rules to be made* | 1. Agree on starting positions and order of service. |
| *by the children* | 2. Play either to 10 or 15 points. Decide if you want a straight win after 9-all or 14-all; or play best of 3. |

Coaching	1. Practise setting up and batting in pairs.
	2. Try out the change-over, so that each player understands his new position before each service.
	3. Practise the service.
	4. Work out a scoring system while allowing players to help each other.

| *Variation* | The receiving team may only play the ball three times on their side of the net before volleying it across. |

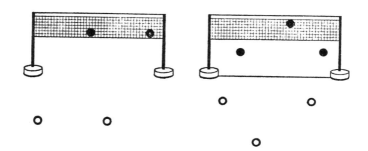

Stage 4
informal Newcombe, 2 v. 2

Stage 5
prisoner ball, 3 v. 3

service area

service area

Stage 6: *4 v. 4*

Stage 7: *6 v. 6*

Introduction to rounders progressions

The rounders skills built up in Stage 1–3 are difficult for young children to learn and should not be attempted until a small ball can be handled with assurance. While these skill practices are being mastered, the children should play the games of Stages 4 and 5. Stages 6, 7 and 8 are similar in difficulty but will not be tackled successfully until the children can use the skills of Stage 3 with ease.

Basic rounders skills:

Bowling

Swing the arm with the ball well back, turning the hip and shoulders to face sideways, with your weight on the back foot. Swing forward forcefully, transferring the weight to the front foot (left foot for right-handed players and vice versa) and rotating the hips and shoulders. Hold the wrist firmly but not stiffly and release the ball forcefully; a jerk in the wrist produces a 'donkey drop', that is, the ball rises sharply instead of moving in a straight line.

Variations in footwork (as they apply to right-handed bowlers)

a. Start with the feet together; step forward with the left foot as the right arm swings forward.

b. Start with the feet together, step forward with the left foot, bring the right foot up behind the left at the same time as the hand holding the ball swings *backward* and the hips and shoulders are rotated backward; then step forward on the left foot and swing the arm forward forcefully, releasing the ball at the moment of greatest acceleration. Follow through in the direction of flight.

Variations in release of the ball

a. In height; the ball may pass the batsman between knee- and head-height.

b. In force.

c. Add spin with the first or fourth fingers.

Common faults in bowling

a. There is no rotation in hips and shoulders.

b. The wrist is allowed to 'give' at the moment of release.

c. The arm and hand are too low or high at release.

d. There is no follow through.

Backstopping

Stand lightly balanced on the toes, ready to move behind the direction of the ball. Hands must be cupped at the ready. Catch the ball, and in one continuous movement swing the body, shoulder and hand to the preferred side and throw over-arm to first post. The more fluent these movements the better. Practise throwing to second, third and fourth posts and to the bowler. Practise using an under-arm throw. (In later stages this will be found to be faster for the shorter distances: for example, fourth post and bowler.)

Common faults in backstopping

a. Lack of concentration.
b. Not knowing where to throw, thus breaking the continuity of the action.
c. Hands not extended towards the ball: no 'give' in arms, wrists and fingers.
d. Stiff body, ankles and feet.

Batting

At first, a bat similar to a cricket bat in shape is recommended; later, a rounders-stick, *light* enough to be swung with ease.

Stand sideways-on to the bowler; swing the bat or stick backwards at shoulder-height as the ball leaves the bowler's hand and forward again in a continuous movement, transferring the weight first to the back, then to the front foot. Step with the front foot in the direction of the ball, turning the hips and shoulders. Hold the bat or stick firmly at the moment of impact. The head should face the ball throughout the movement. Judge how fast the ball is coming towards you.

Variations at the moment of impact

a. The face of the bat or side of the stick determines direction.
b. The ball can be hit early or late; that is, slightly in front of or behind the body.

Common faults in batting

a. A lack of concentration.
b. There is no adjustment to the height of the ball.
c. There is 'give' in the wrist.
d. The eyes are closed at the moment of impact.

Fielding

Run so that you face the direction of the ball; bend at the hips, knees and ankles. Reach out with both hands or one hand and bring the ball in towards the body; turn if necessary, as you straighten up, and throw over-arm in one continuous action.

Progression of rounders   Stage **1**
Name of game   **1** and **1**

Equipment	One rubber or rounders ball between two children.
Play	*Skill practices* 1. Bowling in both directions. 2. Bowling and backstopping; return over-arm throw. 3. Rolling; return over-arm throw. 4. Rolling competition, both children starting from the same spot. 5. Rolling or throwing at an angle to a fielder. 6. Throwing over-arm or under-arm in both directions.
Rules made by the teacher	1. 'Beat your own record' activities, for example: increase your distance with every correct bowling backstopping/throwing action.
Rules to be made by the children	1. Decide who starts bowling and who backstopping. 2. Decide how many balls to play before changing over.
Coaching	See the notes on basic skills on pp. 118–20.

Progression of rounders   Stage **2**
Name of game   **practice in threes**

Equipment	One rubber or rounders ball between three children; a line to mark the front of the bowling base.
Play	No. 1 is the bowler, no. 2 backstop, no. 3 first-post fielder. No. 1 bowls; no. 2 catches the ball and in one continuous action throws to no. 3, either over-arm or under-arm; no. 3 passes to no. 1 under-arm.

Rules made by the teacher	Change over positions in this order: bowler to back-stop to fielder.
Rules to be made by the children	1. Decide the number of balls to be bowled by each bowler. 2. Decide on starting positions.
Coaching	1. Bowler: use the correct bowling action (see notes on p. 118). 2. Backstop: observe the hands and eyes of the bowler, move behind the direction of the ball; catch and throw in one continuous action. 3. Fielder: be ready to move behind the direction of the ball. 4. All players: change over without fuss.
Variations	1. The fielder may stand in the position of third or fourth post. 2. An extra child may make a second fielder, standing in the position of third post. No. 3 then throws the ball to no. 4 who returns the ball to the bowler. (NOTE: this slows up the practice considerably.)

Progression of rounders   Stage 3
Name of game   **practice in fours**

Equipment	One rubber or rounders ball, one bat or stick between four children, lines to mark the front of the batting and bowling base.
Play	No. 1 is the bowler, no. 2 the batsman, no. 3 the backstop, no. 4 the fielder. 1. Count the number of hits made. 2. Count the number of times the backstop catches the ball. 3. Count good and no-balls.
Rules made by the teacher	1. No-ball rules: The ball must pass the batsman not higher than the top of the head nor lower than the knees. It must not be directed at the body of the batsman. It must reach the batsman. It must be delivered with a continuous under-arm action.

It must not be wide (out of reach) or pass the batsman on his non-hitting side.

2. The batsman must try to hit *every* ball.

Rules to be made by the children
1. Decide who starts in each position.
2. Decide on the number of balls to be bowled.
3. Devise a system of individual scores.

Coaching
1. Batsman: see p. 119. Experiment with hitting in different directions.
2. Backstop: stand behind the position of the bat or stick, *not* behind the batsman; stand so that you can see the bowler.
3. Bowler: consider the no-ball rules; concentrate quietly before every delivery.
4. Fielder: be ready to move instantly behind the direction of the ball.

Variations
1. The fielder may field from the third-post position.
2. A second fielder may be added.

Progression of rounders   Stage **4**
Name of game
5-a-side kicking or throwing rounders

Equipment
One football size 4; four posts; a marked-out square if possible.

Play
The bowler rolls (throws) the ball to the batsman who kicks (throws) it *within* the square; he runs round the outside of the four posts in turn and may stop at each one. He scores a rounder if he reaches fourth post. The fielders field the ball and throw it to the bowler, who must touch his line with one foot and call 'Stop'. Any fielder running between the posts at this moment is 'out'. Batsmen may start running on as soon as the ball has left the bowler's hands. Any number of batsmen may stop at any post.

Rules made by the teacher
1. The ball must not be kicked or thrown outside the square.
2. The ball must not be missed deliberately by the batsmen.
3. Batsmen must run *outside* the posts.

Rules to be made 1. Decide whether the ball is to be rolled or throw
by the children   again if the batsman missed it *unintentionally*.
2. Decide on the length of the innings: for example,
   each batsman has *one* turn.
3. Decide on the position of each player before you
   begin.
4. Who is the captain of each team?
5. If a fielder catches the ball, should the batsman be
   allowed to carry on or not?

Coaching 1. Remind the children that the captains *together*
   decide whether a rounder has been scored or not.
   If they quarrel, the teacher decides.
2. Encourage the batsman to run as soon as he has
   kicked or thrown the ball.
3. Batsmen should run and not dawdle between posts.
4. Encourage strong kicks or throws in different
   directions.
5. Fielders stand back for a good player, come closer
   in for a less good one.

Variations 1. The batsman is 'out' if he runs inside a post.
2. If there is little space beyond the square, the space
   behind the batsman may be used for kicking or
   throwing.

Progression or rounders   Stage **5**
Name of game
6-a-side dodge-ball rounders

Equipment One football size 4; four posts; a marked-out square,
if possible, and a circle within the square.

Play The batting team is divided into pairs; no. 1 kicks or
throws the ball within the square, then runs without
stopping round the *outside* of the four posts, calling
'Stop' when he *touches* fourth post. As soon as the
ball has been thrown by the bowler, no. 2 runs
inside the circle. The fielders and bowler field the
ball and run into their positions outside the circle
and aim to hit the dodger below the knees before
his partner calls 'Stop'. The batting team scores one
rounder if the dodger is not hit.

| *Rules made by* | 1. The dodger cannot be hit outside the circle. The |
| *the teacher* | fielders must not step inside the circle. |

<table>
<tr><td>Rules made by
the teacher</td><td>

1. The dodger cannot be hit outside the circle. The fielders must not step inside the circle.
2. The batsman must not throw or kick the ball outside the square.
3. If the ball is caught by a fielder, no rounder may be scored, and both players are 'out'.

</td></tr>
</table>

Rules made by
the teacher

1. The dodger cannot be hit outside the circle. The fielders must not step inside the circle.
2. The batsman must not throw or kick the ball outside the square.
3. If the ball is caught by a fielder, no rounder may be scored, and both players are 'out'.

Rules to be made
by the children

1. Who is the captain of each team?
2. Decide on the positions of each player round the circle before you begin.
3. Decide whether the ball is to be rolled or thrown again if the batsman missed it *unintentionally*.
4. Decide on the length of the innings: for example, each batsman has *one* turn.

Coaching

1. Quick fielding or positioning round the circle.
2. Children should guard a section of the circle, but should keep on the move round their area.
3. Quick passing round the circle.
4. The runner must not stop; he must call clearly.

Variation

1. No circle. The dodger may run anywhere within the square. The fielders must pass swiftly between each other and keep near the dodger. They must not run with the ball.
2. Variation of the dodger's rule: if the dodger steps outside the circle, no rounder is scored.
3. If the dodger *catches* the ball, he and his partner score a rounder.

Progression of rounders   Stage **6**
Name of game   **6-a-side Danish rounders**

Equipment

Either one tennis ball or one bat and one rounders ball; four posts to mark a square; one hoop or chalk circle.

Play

The bowler tosses the ball up, the batsman *either* hits the tennis ball with the open palm *or* the rounders ball with a bat; he starts running round the posts and may stop at any one. The fielders return the ball to the bowler in his hoop who calls 'Stop'. Any player running between bases is 'out'.

Rules made by *the teacher*	1. Several batsmen may be out at any time. 2. Only one ball is tossed, the batsman must run whether he hits or misses. 3. The ball must be hit into the field of play. 4. Batsmen may pass each other. 5. A batsman can be caught out.
Coaching	1. The ball should be tossed above head-height, but not too high. 2. The fielders should back each other up.

Progression of rounders   Stage 7
Name of game   6-a-side circular rounders

Equipment	One rounders ball; six bats or sticks, four posts, a marked-out square.
Play	The bowler bowls to the batsman who, whether he hits or misses, immediately starts running round the outside of all four posts in turn, touching no. 4. The fielders throw the ball to first post, who passes to second post, who passes to third post, who passes to fourth post where the fielder calls 'Stop'. A rounder is scored if the batsman reaches fourth post before the ball.
Rules made by *the teacher*	1. Each post-fielder must touch his post with the ball in his hand before throwing on. 2. No-ball rules must be observed. 3. If a player hits a no-ball, he must run. 4. The ball must be hit into or across the square and not behind the player.
Rules to be made *by the children*	1. Who is the captain? Who is the umpire? 2. Decide on positions of players and batting order. 3. Agree on an 'obstruction' rule. 4. Agree on length of innings: for example, the teams change over after each player has had one turn. 5. Decide how a player may be 'out'.
Coaching	1. Each post fielder must be alert and calm. Encourage continuous movements: catching, touching the post and throwing on.

2. The fielders must back each other up.
3. The batsman need only touch fourth post; he can use his hand or bat or stick. He cannot score if he runs inside a post.

Variations

1. The fourth-post fielder throws to the bowler who calls 'Stop'.
2. If the passing is poor, the children may agree on a system of points scoring, for example: 1 point if the ball reaches second post, 2 points if it reaches third post and 3 points for fourth post. The captains keep the score for their side, and add their fielding and batting scores together.
3. The square may be enlarged for older children.
4. The batsman may attempt two rounders.

Progression of rounders

Name of game

Stage **8**

6- or 7-a-side passing rounders

Equipment

Rounders pitch; one rounders ball; six to seven bats.

Play

The bowler bowls the ball to the batsman who, whether he hits or misses, starts running round the four posts, touching the last one and calling 'Stop'. The fielders pass the ball to the bowler who exchanges the ball with first-, second-, third- and fourth-post fielders in turn. If the batsman reaches fourth post before the bowler catches the ball from the fourth-post fielder, he has scored a rounder.

Rules made by the teacher

1. The post fielders must touch their posts with the ball in their hands.
2. A batsman may be caught out.

Rules to be made by the children

1. Choose your best catcher to be bowler.
2. Devise a system of scoring if the complete game is rather slow.
3. Agree on an 'obstruction' rule.

Coaching

1. The bowler and the post fielders need to be alert and should pass in continuous actions.

Variations

1. Use the teacher's rules for circular rounders.
2. The batsman must run twice round all the posts.

126

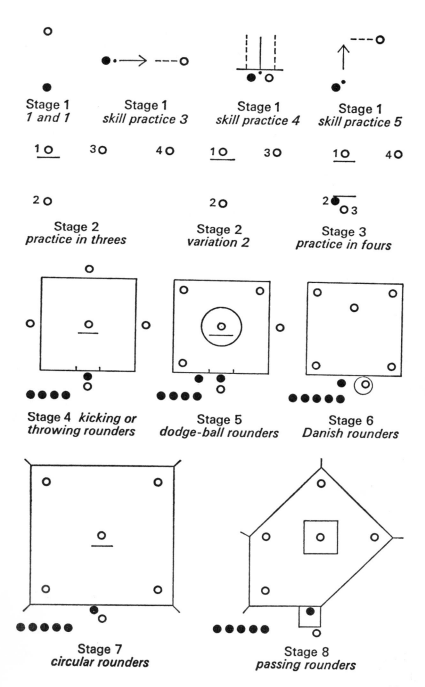

Stage 1
1 and 1

Stage 1
skill practice 3

Stage 1
skill practice 4

Stage 1
skill practice 5

Stage 2
practice in threes

Stage 2
variation 2

Stage 3
practice in fours

Stage 4 *kicking or throwing rounders*

Stage 5
dodge-ball rounders

Stage 6
Danish rounders

Stage 7
circular rounders

Stage 8
passing rounders

Introduction to cricket and stool-ball progressions

As the development of these two games is very similar, they have been treated together. The techniques are quite different and a description of the main points precedes the stages of the games. At Stage 2 stool-ball is given as a variation; Stage 3 is described in terms of cricket and Stage 4 in terms of stool-ball. Eleven-a-side games of either cricket or stool-ball are not recommended as class activities for the reasons given in chapters 1 and 2, and because they require much time.

Basic cricket skills:

Batting

a. The batsman should stand sideways to the wicket, as in rounders or for the forehand drive in tennis. The left toe may point diagonally forward to the right (the 'off' side of a cricket pitch).
b. The grip is unnatural and must be practised from the beginning so that it becomes habitual. Pick up the bat by the grip with the palms of the hands facing in opposite directions, right hand below the left. Now turn the left hand towards the body, until the knuckles face obliquely forward to the right.
c. Lift the bat backward so that the wrists keep *in advance* of the bat. Swing the bat keeping the wrists forward.
(NOTE: the left hand is more important than the right; the elbows must keep out and away from the body; the left foot should move in the direction of the ball.)

Bowling

Use a hard rubber ball (or a cricket ball at the teacher's discretion).
a. Hold the ball comfortably in the fingers, not the palm. A right-handed bowler should step with the left foot firmly forward and hold the left leg straight, but not stiffly, so that it acts as a pivot. Swing the right arm in a large circle; look forward to the spot you want to aim at; release the ball with a flick of the wrist (but elbows *not* moving) at the highest point.
b. Try this again, using the left arm stretched out and pointing in the direction of the flight of the ball. Cut the left arm away sharply as the right hand releases the ball. Look over your left shoulder and straight at the spot you aim at. Experiment with a run up.
c. Experiment with the release of the ball. Vary the pace of the ball, using the wrist with more or less force. Vary the direction very very slightly. Give spin to the ball with the first or fourth fingers.

Wicket-keeping

If you have proper gloves, point your fingers *downward* and let the ball come towards you. Move behind the direction of the ball, with one foot close to the wicket for stumping.

If no gloves are used, catch in the usual manner, hands reaching towards the ball and bringing it in towards the body. (When cricket balls are used the wicket-keeper should wear gloves.)

Fielding

This is similar to rounders, but since a cricket ball is heavier it can hurt more. Use rubber and tennis balls until children dare catch a hard ball. Good fielding chiefly consists in:

a. Getting behind the direction of the ball and reaching out low enough with both hands; then stretching up and throwing the ball in one continuous movement.

b. If the fielder starts at an angle to the ball, he must stretch out one hand. Courage and concentration are crucial.

Basic stool-ball skills

Batting

A stool-ball bat is heavy; it has a long handle and a round, flat face with curved back. The batsman should use one hand only and hold the bat by the end of the handle. He should stand sideways to the wicket with the bat facing the bowler and covering the wicket. The batsman should stand astride the crease and make sure he can swing the bat without touching the wicket.

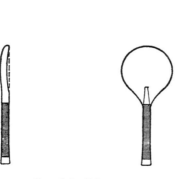

Stool-ball bat   **Stool-ball wicket**

Bowling

Use a hard rubber or rounders ball.

As for rounders but with two exceptions: (i) the ball may be directed straight at the batsman; (ii) the face of the wicket is small and relatively high. Accurate under-arm bowling is necessary.

Wicket-keeping

Because of the size and shape of the wicket, the wicket-keeper must crouch down or stand at one side of the wicket; he must remember that the ball must touch *the face* of the wicket to get a batsman out.

Progression of cricket and stool-ball   Stage 1
Name of game   **pairs**

Equipment	*One rubber or tennis ball between two children.*
Play	Skill practices in pairs: 1. Throwing and fielding from alternate ends. 2. Bowling from both ends. 3. Bowling and wicket-keeping; over-arm return throw.
Coaching	(See pp. 128–30.) Use under-arm bowling with younger juniors.) Aim at a cricket wicket painted on a wall, or at a spring wicket, or at stumps, increasing the distance as your skill increases. Coach *under-arm* bowling first.

Progression of cricket and stool-ball   Stage 2
Name of game
French cricket or stool-ball in fours

Equipment	One bat or one cricket-bat shape; one ball between four players.
Play	Three bowlers/fieldsmen and one batsman: the bowlers try to hit the batsman's feet and legs below the knee; the batsman uses his bat to protect himself.
Rules to be made by the children	1. Decide who is the first batsman and how you change round. No player should bat too long or miss a turn.

Coaching	1. Each bowler is a fielder as well and must field in his zone.
	2. Under-arm bowling (informal).
	3. If a cricket-bat shape is used, use the correct grip.
	4. The bowlers can pass between each other before bowling.
	5. The batsman should concentrate on the ball and face it.

Variations	1. Use a stool-ball bat and wicket.
	2. Use a rounders bat or playbat.
	3. The batsman must keep his feet still.

Progression of cricket and stool-ball   Stage **3**
Name of game
non-stop cricket or stool-ball   (A)   **3** v. **3**

Equipment

Five stumps or one stool-ball post and two stumps; one ball, preferably hard rubber; one cricket-bat shape or stool-ball bat; batsman's and bowler's crease marked.

Play

There are two teams of three: one bowler, one batsman and one wicket-keeper; three fielders. All the children co-operate. The first team change over in order after each batsman is 'out'; when all three are out, they change with the three fielders. Both individual and team scores are kept. The bowler bowls the ball; if the batsman hits it, he must run *round* the stump to his left and return to his crease as fast as possible. Meanwhile the fielders throw the ball to the bowler who can bowl again whether the batsman has returned or not.

Ways of getting a batsman out: *a.* bowled *b.* caught. (NOTE: the batsman cannot be 'run out'.)

Coaching

Batsman
1. Hold the cricket-bat shape correctly; hit vigorously.
2. Run immediately, even if the ball has barely touched the bat.

Bowler
Keep calm; concentrate on your aim; bowl underarm.

Fielders

Watch the face of the bat; move instantly; return the ball to the bowler, *not* the wicket.

Variations   Allow the batsman to be run out, that is, allow the wicket to be touched by a fielder. (This will result in constant changing over and accelerates the game too much for *beginners*.)

Progression of cricket and stool-ball   Stage **4**
Name of game
1 team non-stop stool-ball or cricket (B)

Equipment   One stool-ball post and two stumps, or five stumps; one ball, one bat; line for a batting crease optional.

Play   The playing positions are numbered as follows: 1—bowler, 2—batsman, 3—wicket-keeper, 4, 5 and 6—fielding positions. The children move round in *order*. Individual scores. The bowler bowls the ball; if the batsman hits it he must run *round* the stump to his left and return as fast as possible to his crease. Meanwhile the fielders field the ball and throw it to the bowler who can bowl again whether the batsman has returned or not. A batsman can be caught, bowled or run out. The *bowler* should call 'out' and everybody moves on to the next position; the next bowler starts bowling as soon as possible.

Rules made by
the teacher

Wicket-keeper
1. Touch the face of the stool-ball post with the ball in your hand, or throw it, to get a batsman out.
2. Bails on cricket stumps are optional; touching a stump should be sufficient at this stage.

Batsman
1. More than one run may be scored off a hit; if a batsman is out on a later run, he may count the score so far.
2. Batsmen must run *round* the stump (not merely touch it with the bat), and return to the crease.

Rules to be made   1. Decide where each player starts.
by the children   2. Should you make a rule for a *maximum* number of runs?

1. The children need to be both calm and alert.
2. Remind children of the order of the positions.
3. The fielders must make up their minds whether to throw to the bowler or wicket-keeper.
4. Remind the batsman that he can score more than one run in the event of an overthrow.

Variations

1. One or two additional fielders can be used. More are not recommended.
2. Use a stool-ball or cricket-ball.

Progression of cricket and stool-ball   Stage 5
Name of game
5-a-side cricket or stool-ball

Equipment

One bat and four stumps or one stool-ball wicket and one stump; one ball between ten players; lines for batting and bowling crease. (The bowling crease can also be marked with a stump.)

Play

One wicket only: one batting team of five players; one fielding team made up of one bowler, one wicket-keeper, three fielders. The aim is to score more runs than the opposing team. Run to the bowler's crease and back to score one run. A batsman is out if he is caught, or run out or bowled.

Rules made by the teacher

1. 'Wide' balls. If these are to be counted, an umpire is needed.
2. Over-arm bowling may be permitted for a cricket game.
3. Allow five balls per over or discuss with children.
4. Bowl from the same end but change the bowler at each over.

Rules to be made by the children

1. Choose a captain, batting order and fielding positions.
2. Should over-arm bowling be allowed?
3. Choose at least two bowlers.

Coaching

1. This can be either a formal or an informal game, depending on skill.
2. If formal, coach correct bowling:
   a. wides

b. stepping over the crease;

if informal, concentrate on getting the batting team out.

<table>
<tr><td>*Variations*</td><td>1. *Either:* allow one run if the batsman, having hit or missed the ball reaches the bowler's crease with his bat; he may walk back;

or: he may score *two* runs if he reaches the batsman's crease again before being out. Make a distinction between walking and running back. The batsman can only be run out at the crease he is running to.</td></tr>
</table>

2. Play 6- or 7-a-side.

Progression of cricket and stool-ball   Stage **6**
Name of game
6-a-side circular cricket or stool-ball

Equipment

One wicket, five stumps, one bowling crease, one batting crease; one ball between twelve children; one bat.

The stumps are arranged in a half-circle, the wicket half-way between the first and fifth stump.

Play

Batting side: one batsman stands in front of the wicket, the other batsmen at their stumps. Fielders: one bowler, one wicket-keeper and four fielders; each fielder needs to know in which position on the batting side he starts. The bowler bowls under-arm; if the batsman hits the ball, *all* the members of the batting side run on one or more places. Runs are scored between the batting crease and the first post. Every batsman must pick up the bat and touch the crease (cricket) or the face of the wicket (stool-ball) and call either 'Yes' if he thinks the next batsman can reach the wicket or 'No' and all stop in position. He may not run on when the bowler has called 'Stop', that is, when the bowler stands ready behind his crease with the ball in his hand. A batsman can be bowled or run out or caught; the captain of the fielding side calls 'Side out' and all change over immediately. Each fielder must remember which stump he was at last.

Coaching

1. The change-over must be smooth and not result in a muddle. This is an excellent game for intelligent children with little skill.
2. The fielders must be alert and decide whether it is better to throw to the wicket-keeper and possibly get the other side out or throw the bowler and stop any further runs.
3. Each batsman must decide if the batsman *behind* him can reach the wicket. He must not forget to touch the wicket, otherwise his run does not count.
4. In the stool-ball game the wicket-keeper may be allowed to touch the incoming batsman with the ball in his hand and so get his side out.
5. Remind the captains that they must keep the score.

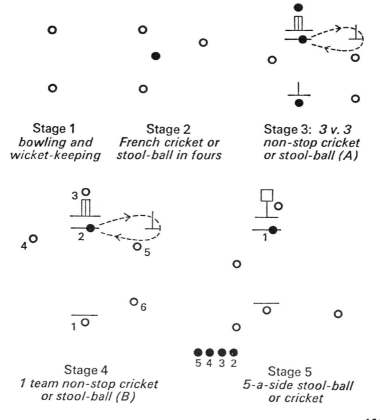

Stage 1
*bowling and
wicket-keeping*

Stage 2
*French cricket or
stool-ball in fours*

Stage 3: *3 v. 3
non-stop cricket
or stool-ball (A)*

Stage 4
*1 team non-stop cricket
or stool-ball (B)*

Stage 5
*5-a-side stool-ball
or cricket*

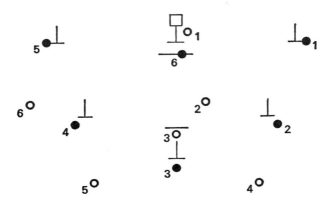

Stage 6
6-a-side
circular stool-ball or cricket

Dodge-ball

Progression of dodge-ball games   Stage **1**
         Name of game   **pairs**

         See 'Aiming at targets', p. 67.

Progression of dodge-ball games   Stage **2**
         Name of game   **2** v. **1**

Equipment	One ball size 3 or 4 between three children.
Play	Aim at the dodger who stands between you. Use over-arm throws and try to hit him below the knees.
Rules made by the teacher	1. Only hits below the knee count.
Rules to be made by the children	1. Decide how to change over. 2. Decide how to score.
Coaching	*The throwers* 1. Pass between you—do not aim with each throw. 2. Do not stand in a line but move round the dodger; try to throw from an unexpected direction. 3. Be ready to field the ball quickly. *The dodger* 1. Always face the child with the ball. 2. Look at the eyes and hands of the child with the ball. 3. Jump with your feet apart.
Variation	Tower-ball (see p. 80, *Variations* 2 and diagram, p. 87).

Progression of dodge-ball games   Stage **3**
         Name of game   **3** v. **1**

Equipment	One ball size 3 or 4 between four children; a marked circle (optional).
Play	Aim at the dodger who stands between you. Use over-arm throws and try to hit him below the knee.
Rules made by the teacher	Only hits below the knee count.

1. Decide how to change over.
2. Decide how to score.
3. Decide if the centre player may catch the ball and thus score or change over.

Coaching

1. You are responsible for fielding one-third of the area round the dodger; keep on your toes and do not let any ball pass you.
2. Keep in your own section and do not run right round the dodger.

Variation

1. 4 v. 1. This is not as good a game as 3 v 1. The balls tends to go backward and forward between one couple of players and the game is not so active.
2. 3 v. 2. This game can be used when there is an odd number of children in the class. The two dodgers must wear bands and have a chalk circle to identify their space.

Larger teams are not recommended.

Progression of dodge-ball games   Stage **4**
Name of game   **three-court dodge-ball**

Equipment

One ball size 4; playground chalk; three braids of one colour and three of another.

Play

The two outside teams try to hit the middle team below the knee.

Rules made by
the teacher

1. Only hits below the knee count.
2. The size of the court: for example, about 8×5 metres.
3. A system of changing round: for example, the courts are numbered and the teams change from 1—2—3—1.
4. Time limit: for example, 2 minutes in each court; or change round after each successful hit; or change round after three hits.

Rules to be made
by the children

1. If a time limit is set, how could you score?
2. Can you think of another way of determining when to change over?
3. What should happen if the ball goes outside the boundaries?

4. Could you make a rule so that the middle court players could *catch* the ball?

Coaching

1. Change over promptly.
2. Start again at once,
    either: after all are in their new court,
        or: immediately one end-player has secured the ball.
3. End-court players: throw the ball so that the players at the other end can catch it.
    If you throw wildly more time will be spent fielding than playing.
4. Middle-court players: keep watching the ball and jump in good time.

Progression of dodge-ball games
Name of game

Stage **5**

two-court dodge-ball **4** v. **4**

Equipment

One large ball; four braids of one colour and four of another; playground chalk.

Play

The two teams try to hit and eliminate each other by throws touching a player below the knee. The two outside players field along their base-line and attack from there so that each team is under fire from two sides. Players eliminated from their court join the outside player and help him attack from the base-line. The ball may be intercepted but, if it is dropped, the player attempting to intercept is eliminated.

Rules made by the teacher

1. Only hits below the knee count.
2. The size of the court: for example, 3.5 × 5 metres.
3. The teams change ends.
    either: after all the players of one side are eliminated,
    or: after two successful hits,
    or: after a time limit.

Rules to be made by the children

1. How should the game be started?
2. Who should collect the ball if it goes outside the boundaries?

139

3. Decide on a rota for the outside player.
4. Supposing the ball touches the ground in your court and then rolls and touches a player, should he be eliminated?

Coaching

1. Watch the ball coming from the other court *or* the outside player; keep turning to face the ball.
2. See if you can intercept it.
3. Pass among each other to confuse your opponents; pass or throw quickly.
4. Do not throw very hard balls; accuracy is more important.
5. Outside players: be alert to move along your line.

Variations

1. The outside player on each team can change over with the first player on his side to be hit.
2. Play 5- or 6-a-side; when several players have been eliminated they could field and attack from the three outside boundaries of their opponents' court.
(NOTE: this is a version of a well-known continental game called Voelkerball.)

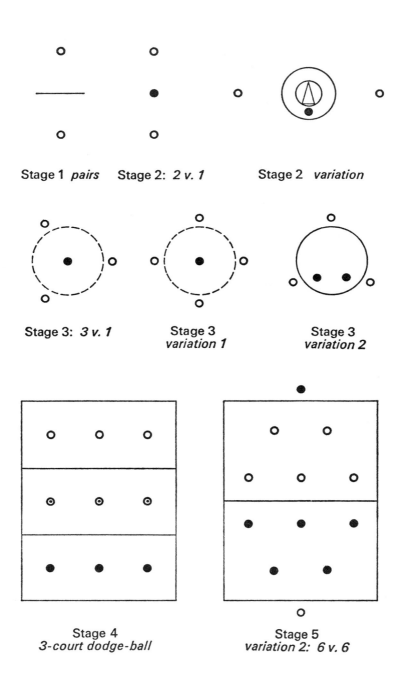

Stage 1 *pairs*   Stage 2: *2 v. 1*   Stage 2 *variation*

Stage 3: *3 v. 1*   Stage 3
                          variation 1

Stage 3
variation 2

Stage 4
3-court dodge-ball

Stage 5
variation 2: 6 v. 6

5 *Running Games*

Non-competitive games

1 *'The pedestrian crossing'* [1]

All children choose whether to drive a motor-car or bus, or to ride a bicycle along the road marked in chalk on the playground. At a signal they gather at the pedestrian crossing which should extend from one side of the playground to the other. The children walk across the crossing. One of them can be the policeman or traffic warden.

2 *'Wind and rain'* [2]

The children run round the playground slowly or quickly. They are the wind which may blow softly or strongly. When the teacher calls 'It rains', they change to jumping over the puddles marked on the playground. The children will enjoy drawing some interesting puddles.

3 *'Lines'* [3]

The children run and jump freely over the lines drawn on the playground. On a signal they quickly stand on one of the lines. There must be at least as many lines as children. Later the teacher may try to catch the children before they reach a line.

4 *'Animals and their lairs'*

The children move about like animals but when the hunter—the teacher—strides across the playground they disappear into their lairs. When they think he has gone away they come out again. Later this game may be played more formally with 'lairs' drawn on the playground, the hunter catching any unwary animals.

[1] Based on p. 53 of *Activity Games* by P. M. Kingston (1954; now out of print).
[2] *ibid.* p. 52.
[3] *ibid.* p. 56.

5 *'The toy shop'*

The toys come out from their cupboards or shelves and begin to move about according to their kind. When the shopkeeper—the teacher—rattles his key in the door, they quickly run to their cupboards or shelves and lie down. Later the teacher may catch the children before they get back to pre-arranged 'cupboards' or 'shelves'.

Group and competitive games

Two points should be noted about group games:
1. Children should never turn directly round and start running in the opposite direction, as this leads to accidents; changes of direction should be made at an angle.
2. A wall should never be 'home' or a target in a running game. Children should not be chased towards a wall.

1 *'The birds'* [1]

The children are divided into groups of equal numbers, each with an empty hoop (the nest). In the centre of the playground a circle is drawn (the field). In it there is an assortment of small apparatus (the food), for example: beanbags, quoits, tied skipping ropes or blocks. The birds fly round the field, dipping and swooping. When the teacher calls 'The farmer has gone to market', the birds carry the food, one piece at a time, from the field to their own nests. The leader of each group counts the food and writes the number in chalk by the hoop. At the next turn the birds try to empty their nests as quickly as possible, returning the food piece by piece to the field. When all the food has been returned, the leader raises his arm.

2 *'The fire brigade game'*

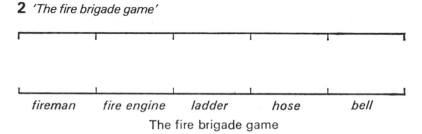

fireman   fire engine   ladder   hose   bell

The fire brigade game

[1] Based on p. 62 of *Games and Activities for Infants* by Margaret Laing (now out of print).

Each group of children is either the fireman or part of his equipment, such as the fire engine, the big ladder, the hose or the bell. The teacher tells a story in which these words occur frequently. The children in each group occupy a section of a long line drawn along one side of the playground. Each time the children hear their object mentioned, they run from their line to another line on the other side of the playground.

When the teacher mentions 'the fire' all run across to the other side of the playground, regardless of which side they happen to be at that moment.

Example of a story

One day, when the *fireman* was standing on the *ladder* cleaning the big *fire-engine*, the telephone *bell* rang. There was a *fire* in the middle of the town. They fixed the *hose* and the *ladder* quickly and all the *firemen* jumped on the *fire-engine* and raced to the *fire* with their *bell* ringing all the way. When they arrived they pulled out the long *ladder* and got the *hose* ready and one of the *firemen* climbed the *ladder* with the *hose*. They could hear the *bells* of a lot more *fire-engines* racing to the *fire*.

Variations
Tell a story about a zoo or a toy shop.

3 *'The trains'*

Small groups of children (not more than four) play 'Follow My Leader'. The leader is the engine, the other children the carriages or wagons. The engine pulls the train quickly or slowly all over the playground. On a signal they all race to their own station which can be marked with chalk or a hoop. See which train gets home first.

Teaching points

a. Make sure all the 'trains' know their 'stations'.
b. Remind the leader of his responsibility for leading his train.
c. Change the leader after each turn of the game.

Variations
a. 'Buses':
The leader is the driver and the children are the passengers.
b. 'Birds on a Farm':
The leader is the mother goose, the children are the goslings. Further variations can be made with: duck and ducklings; chickens and chicks; turkey and turkey chicks.

4 *'Tom Tiddler's ground' or 'Chinese wall'*

The catchers stand in a part of the playground marked off by, for example, two lines. The children try to cross the area between the lines without being caught.

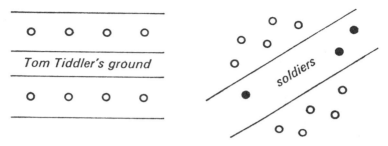

'Tom Tiddler's ground' or 'Chinese wall'

Teaching points

a. Tom Tiddler or the soldiers on the wall may not cross the lines.
b. The children must not stop within the lines but must cross from one side to the other quickly.
c. Once caught, they put on a braid and help the catchers.

Chasing and dodging games in pairs

1 *The children choose partners*

Half of them run round the playground, the other half wait behind a line each holding a braid in his hand. On a signal they catch any partner. Both children take hold of the braid and skip round together. Change over.

Teaching points

a. Do not push each other.
b. Change over quickly.

Variation

When one child has caught another they stand still. In this way the slower children go on running longer.

2 *'Mary and her lamb'* [1]

'Follow My Leader' in pairs. The leader is Mary, the other child her

[1] Based on p. 67 of *Games and Activities for Infants* by Margaret Laing.

lamb. Mary can move in any way she likes, the lamb copying all the actions. On a signal Mary turns round and chases her lamb; when caught, both children stand still. The teacher can count aloud up to 10, when all the children stop running. He can see how many lambs are still free. Change over.

Teaching points

a. It would be sensible if all the Marys or all the lambs had a braid on, but not both.
b. Listen for the signal.
c. Do not bump into each other.
(NOTE: the teacher must be quite firm about this.)

3 'Catch your partner's tail'

Each child tucks his braid in the back of his shorts or pants; only 2–3 inches of braid are tucked in, the rest hangs freely down the back. Each child tries to catch his partner's braid without losing his own. When one of them has succeeded, they change over. A time limit can be set or each child may lose three 'lives', that is, lose his braid three times.

Teaching points

a. Do not tuck too much of your braid into your shorts.
b. Swiftly dodge from side to side and keep facing your partner. Do not run away.
c. Pretend you are dodging and reaching out to one side, but make your real attack on the opposite side.
d. Reach well out with either hand to catch your partner's braid.
e. Do not barge into or push your partner.
To set a time limit, the teacher can slowly count aloud to 10.
He can ask one of the following questions:
1. Who caught their partner's braid?
2. Who did not lose their own braid?
3. Who caught their partner's but kept their own braid?
4. Who lost one, two, or three 'lives'?

Variations

a. One braid between two children, no. 1 child tucks his braid in his shorts or pants, no. 2 tries to catch it. Change over, either after a time limit or whenever the braid has been caught.
b. Either the basic game or variation *a.:* Change partners at a signal.

c. A group game: one group—for example, the blues—are the catchers who try to secure as many braids as possible from the other groups in a given time.

d. A snowball-type game: one child (or more) wears his braid in the usual way, all the other children have their braids tucked into their shorts or pants. When a child is caught, he puts his braid on in the usual way and joins in the catching.

(NOTE: do not carry on too long as this game can get boring very quickly. Choose a new starter from those who did not lose their braids. A time limit can be set.)

4 *Dodging in pairs, facing each other*

There is no major game in which this is directly applicable, but it is a necessary preliminary to the following games because it teaches children to be observant and adjust to and anticipate an opponent's movements in the simplest possible form. This stage should, therefore, not be prolonged.

No. 1 child is the dodger, no. 2 tries to keep within arm's length. Both children must stop dead at a signal, no. 2 reaching out to see if he can still touch his partner.

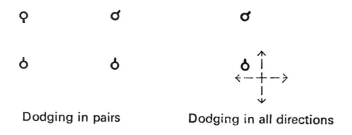

Dodging in pairs   Dodging in all directions

Teaching points

a. Dodger: move forward, backward, jump up, bob down or from side to side and change your speed.

b. Consider your partner; keep trying to outwit him: for example, try to pretend you are going one way, then go another.

c. Marker: anticipate your partner's moves by looking at his feet and eyes.

d. Both: listen for the signal and stop immediately.

e. Use small quick movements on the ball of the foot. Keep your knees relaxed and change your weight rapidly.

5 *Dodging in pairs*

No.1 stands in front of no. 2, who dodges behind him. No. 2 starts moving, no. 1 tries to keep up with no. 2. At the signal both stop dead, no. 1 reaching out to see if he is still within reach of no. 2.

Teaching points

a. No. 2 dodge as before, move to either side of, in front or behind your partner.
b. Change speed rapidly: for example, move very fast, then stop dead unexpectedly, letting your partner over-shoot.
c. No. 1 half turn your head and stand a little to the side of your partner; look out of the corner of your eye; be very quick to change direction and anticipate your partner's changes of direction.

Common faults

a. Moving too long in one direction.
b. Slip-steps instead of quick, small steps.
c. Not using all the space round you.
d. Using the same speed all the time.

6 *Dodging in larger groups*

1 v. 3 in a circle

No. 1 is the catcher, nos, 2, 3, and 4 hold hands in a circle; they are the dodgers. No. 1 tries to touch no. 2 on the back. If this proves too difficult, he can touch his hands or arms.

Teaching points

a. No. 1: use quick, short steps, changing direction and speed rapidly; reach out with your finger-tips and extend your whole arm.
b. Nos. 2, 3, and 4: hold hands tightly or use hand-wrist hold; no. 2 keep opposite no. 1 and follow his every move with your eyes and feet.
c. Make up your minds how you will change over.

Variation
1 v. 4. No. 1 may catch either nos. 2 or 3.

1 v. 3 in a line

No. 1 is the wolf; no. 2 is Mother Goose, holding her arms ('wings') outstretched, facing the wolf. The goslings hold tightly to Mother

Goose's hips, one behind the other. If the wolf touches the last gosling on the back he has caught his dinner.

Teaching points

a. The wolf: dodge quickly from side to side, reaching out with arms and fingers extended. Outwit the geese.

b. Mother Goose: keep facing the wolf; never let him get past you; flap your wings.

c. The goslings: hold on tightly to the hips of the child in front.

d. Decide how you will change round.

Variations

a. For five children have one more gosling.

(NOTE: this line is really too long and often breaks; however, it is useful when there is an odd number of children.)

b. For three children have only one gosling.

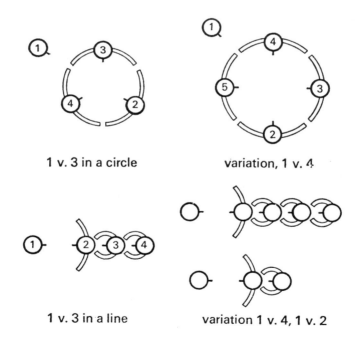

1 v. 3 in a circle variation, 1 v. 4

1 v. 3 in a line variation 1 v. 4, 1 v. 2

Class games

1 *'He' or 'tag' games*

One catcher for every ten children; the catcher wearing a braid.
See how many children you can 'tag' while I count 10.
(NOTE: everybody must keep moving.)

Variations
a. After every turn of the game, hand your braid to the nearest child
who becomes the catcher.
b. After every turn of the game hand your braid to a child who was
not 'tagged'.
c. Have one catcher from each group of ten children: for example,
one blue, one red, one green and one yellow. After every turn of
the game hand the braid to another member of your own team.

Teaching points
a. The catchers: 'tag' very lightly, do not bump the other children.
b. Keep changing direction so that you catch children unexpectedly.
c. All the catchers keep an eye on each other so that you run in
opposite directions and chase the children towards each other.
d. The other children: keep moving and look out for the catchers.

1. *'Pass the braid'*

For every ten players choose one catcher, who is given a braid or other
object. The catchers try to pass the braid on, the other children dodging and evading them. Any player who is tagged *must* stop, take the
braid and try to pass it on as fast as possible. Stop frequently and
choose new catchers from those not tagged.

3 *Couple 'tags'*

a. The class is divided in pairs, holding hands; there is one catcher
for every five couples. 'Tag' and change over with any child
'tagged'.
b. All the class is divided in pairs. To every five couples there is one
'tagging' couple who try to 'tag' as many couples as they can while
the teacher counts 10.
c. All members of the class move about individually. Start with no
fewer than two catchers, and three or four catchers for a large
class. The first catchers 'tag' one other child each, then run in
pairs, each couple then 'tags' one other child, runs as a threesome,

then 'tags' a fourth child. The four children break up into two couples. Both couples start again, catching a third and then a fourth child and dividing up. This game can be very slow in starting if there are too few catchers at the beginning. A tight area limitation is recommended. Stop frequently, and start again using children who are still 'free' as catchers.

4 *Release 'tags'*

For this game, an area limitation is necessary. The area can be smaller for older children; size depends on numbers. One catcher for every ten players.

a. 'The Sun and Jack Frost' (for small children). There should be one Sun (yellow braid) and one Jack Frost (blue braid) for every ten players. The Jack Frosts freeze the children by their magic touch. The children must stand still until 'thawed' by one of the Suns.

Teaching point

The Suns must look round swiftly to 'thaw' the children who are 'frozen'.

b. The catchers 'tag' as many children as possible, counting how many they can 'tag' while the teacher counts up to 10. When 'tagged' the children jump up and down until released by the touch of any 'free' child.

Teaching points

i. The 'tagged' children should keep jumping up and down.
ii. Change the catchers frequently, comparing individual scores.

Variations

a. The 'tagged' children stand with their feet wide apart and are released when a 'free' child crawls under their legs.
b. The 'tagged' children stand with their arms out, the 'free' children release them by running a complete circle round them under their arms.
c. The 'tagged' children curl up on the ground with their heads well tucked in. The 'free' children jump over them to release them.
d. The 'tagged' children stay in prone kneeling positions until the 'free' children release them by putting their hands on their backs and jumping over them.

6   *Sports Day Practices*

Sports Day programmes can be divided into formal events (which will lead later to adult events and should be coached with this in mind), and informal events. One customary event, the three-legged race, is not recommended as it is too dangerous. Some traditional events, such as potato and egg-and-spoon races are quite difficult for infants, but may be fun for 7- to 8-year-olds. They can be played as relay races or individually and must be practised so that children become accustomed to them. Sack races must also be practised with sacks that are large enough but not so big that the children cannot manipulate them. In hopping races, children should be allowed to change feet frequently, but if they put both feet down simultaneously they are eliminated. Children can skip in hoops as well as in skipping ropes, and a new race might be a running race, throwing or bouncing a ball at agreed heights and intervals. 'Back-to-front' or 'crab' races might perhaps be included, such as races on all fours, moving backward or sideways. The distance must be quite short, about 10 metres.

Obstacle races depend on the ingenuity of the teachers who organize them. They should include getting over, under and through obstacles; jumping, balancing, sprinting round obstacles; moving from one obstacle to another (for example, a series of hoops); touching high objects and some aiming event. Each obstacle should be quite easy to negotiate and not more than five or six should be used in a race. There should be an element of surprise present, which precludes any practising beforehand. In some schools parents' races are traditional and obstacle races are more fun than straight sprinting.

All the children in an infant school should take part in the school sports, but heats should be held before Sports Day to eliminate most children in all events except sprinting. Heats for sprints take little time to run off on the day and give each child an opportunity to be 'in' an event. Relay races should not be expected of infants; they must be specially practised with older children as they do not normally form part of the programme. Teachers will have double duties to perform as starters, judges, looking after equipment as well as their classes.

A programme for infants might include: sprints (about 40–50 metres), hopping races, skipping races, bowling-hoop races, back-to-front race, and obstacle race. Juniors need in addition more formal events: throwing a rounders or cricket ball (on a pitch marked as in the diagram at the foot of p. 154), high jumping (provided a proper jumping pit is available), shuttle relay races and perhaps some aiming event.)

A dilemma arises over the classification of entries.

As the first part of this book showed, children vary greatly in stature, maturity, rate of development, skill and ability. Classification by chronological age gives great advantage to the most mature and/or the strongest children. The older the children, the more this is true. However, strength differs little between girls and boys in the primary school, so that sprints and relay races could well be mixed events. High jumping favours the thin, long-legged child whether boy or girl. Only the throwing events should be single sex (see p. 24). An additional event might well be some aiming competition, especially if targets on a wall can be used. For example, points can be given for hitting concentric circles and the distance from the target can be increased with each heat (see diagram, p. 156). Thus, speed, strength, overcoming the force of gravity and accurate aiming can be tested, which give a reasonable spread of skill. An obstacle race may, in addition, demand agility and perhaps ingenuity. Juniors should not be allowed to enter for more than two or three events so that many children have an opportunity to win. At least four groups should be formed for each event. Each school must make up its own mind whether groups should be mixed or single sex.

Coaching for sports day

This is necessary for all events, except obstacle races, so that children understand the rules, starting lines and order of events. Heats should give all the children who elect to enter for an event an equal initial chance, but only finals should take place on the actual day. By completing heats earlier, children become aware of procedure so that all the finalists know their events thoroughly.

1 *Sprints*

These can be run for boys and girls together or separately. An example of distances is as follows:

    8 years or group 4 — 50 metres
    9 years or group 3 — 60 metres
    10 years or group 2 — 70 metres
    11 years or group 1 — 80 metres

Sprints

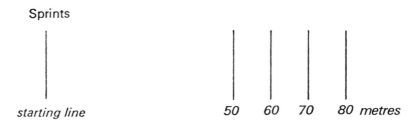

starting line   50   60   70   80 metres

a. Standing start with children 1 metre apart behind a line; starting and finishing lines should be clearly marked.

b. *Feet*
Straight lines should be marked out on the playground or field for children to practise running along them. Their feet should be placed on either side of the lines, pointing straight forward and not turned out or in. Practise in pairs, children watching each other.

c. *Rhythm*
The children should practise running fairly quickly but not racing. Each child will need to become aware of his own rhythm. As children run faster, their strides will lengthen.

d. The elbows should be slightly bent and the fists closely clenched, moving from the thigh to about elbow-height. The arms move in opposition to the legs. Practise in pairs.

2 *Distance-throwing of a rounders or cricket ball*

The same marking as for the sprints, but lines closer to the starting line than 50 metres are recommended. The children should work in pairs, each child marking the place where his partner's ball hit the ground either with chalk or a braid. The best of three tries is a good idea, the children throwing alternately. The children should be fairly well matched, so that competition against each other is fair.

Throwing for distance

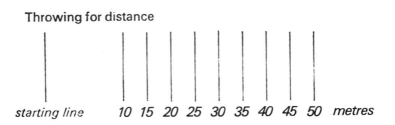

starting line   10 15 20 25 30 35 40 45 50   metres

a. Throw the ball at an angle of 45 degrees; a higher or lower ball will not succeed in reaching the same distance for the same force expended.

b. A run-up to the starting line should be permitted but the forward foot must not cross the starting line until the ball has left the thrower's hand. The teacher should be strict about this. During the follow-through the line may be crossed.

c. The opposite foot to the throwing hand should be in front.

d. The elbow should be brought well back and extended forward really forcefully with the wrist firm and fingers pointing in the direction of the throw.

e. Children should practise with the correct balls right from the beginning.

3 *High jumping.*

This event should depend entirely on the availability of a jumping pit with the children using a scissor technique from the side. Landings should never be made on slippery grass or hard concrete. Even a mat is not sufficient protection and nasty accidents can result.

Scissor jumps

a. Find out which foot you like to take off from. If it is a right foot, then run from the left side, if the left foot, then run from the right side.

b. Lift the foot nearest the rope as you take off from the other foot. The foot nearest the rope is the one you land on.

c. Swing your two legs up as straight as possible, one after the other over the rope. Pay special attention to seeing that your knees and ankles are fully stretched.

d. Lift your seat up by swinging your arms in opposition to your feet and lean well forward.

4 *Shuttle relay*

Batons may be used but flags in house colours look rather fun. This is not an adult race, and teachers should not spent an undue amount of time practising the take-over of the baton.

a. The batons must change hands behind, not in front of a given line; the children not taking over and next in line should stand well back, perhaps behind a second line.

b. The child due to run next should extend his right hand and grasp the baton firmly above the hand of the child racing towards him. There should be no juggling except to move the grip down a fraction so that the next child can carry out the same manoeuvre. Two hands are better than one for changing the grip.

c. Children should be ready to run at top speed and be mentally prepared to let go of the baton. This may be more difficult than to grasp it.

5 *Aiming events*

Under-arm or over-arm throws can be used. The children can practise during playtime. Lines at 5–10 metres from the targets can be drawn. Additional starting-lines can be added as required.

Example 3: cricket targets (a spring wicket or three stumps)

Over-arm or under-arm bowling action can be used with starting-lines at 12, 15, and 18 metres from the target. The ball may hit the

Example 1: concentric circles

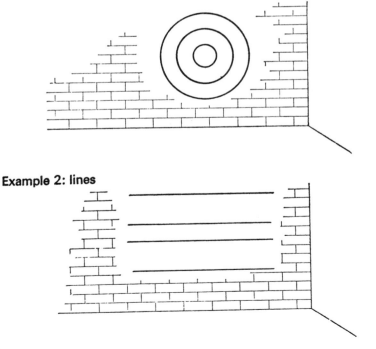

Example 2: lines

ground once, but no point is scored unless the target is hit. Five points are awarded for hitting the middle stump, 3 points for either of the others.

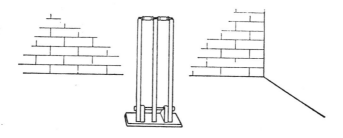

Example 4: a skittle or two or more blocks

Under-arm throwing is more likely to bring success. Starting distances should be 5–10 metres away.

Example of a coaching lesson in preparation for Sports Day

a. Free practice for sprinting.
b. Class practice: sprinting, paying attention to footwork, arms and rhythm.
c. Group work: high jumping; throwing for distance; aiming at a target.
d. Relay practice.

Central Advisory Council for Education (England) (1963) *Half our Future* (The Newsom Report). London: HMSO

Central Advisory Council for Education (England) (1967) *Children and their Primary Schools* (The Plowden Report). London: HMSO.

Cooper, A. (1982) *The development of Games Skills: A scheme of work for teachers.* Oxford: Blackwell.

Department of Education and Science (1972) *Movement: Physical Education in the Primary Years.* London: HMSO.

Department of Health and Social Security (1981) *Report on Health and Social Subjects 21* Sub-committee on Nutritional Surveillance: second report. London: HMSO.

Dunn, M. (1970) *Games Activities for Juniors.* Glasgow: Blackie.

Evans, D.A. (1984) *Teaching Athletics 8–13.* London: Hodder and Stoughton.

Knapp, B. (1977) *Skill in Sport: Attainment of proficiency* (new edition). London: Routledge and Kegan Paul.

Laban, R. (1975) *Modern Educational Dance* (3rd edition). Plymouth: Macdonald and Evans.

Lovell, K. (1973) *Educational Psychology and Children* (11th edition). London: Hodder and Stoughton.

Maulden, E. and Redfern, H.B. (1981) *Games Teaching* (2nd edition). Plymouth: Macdonald and Evans.

Parratt, A.L. (1982) *Indoor Games and Activities: A comprehensive guide to the teaching of games skills to pupils of 7 to 13 years.* London: Hodder and Stoughton.

Piaget, J. (1932) *The Moral Judgment of the Child.* London: Routledge and Kegan Paul; also (1977) Harmondsworth: Penguin Books.

Piaget, J. (1950) *The Psychology of Intelligence.* London: Routledge and Kegan Paul.

Rona, R.J. and Altman, D.C. (1977) 'National Study of Health and Growth: Standards of attained height, weight and triceps skinfold in English children 5-11 years old'; *Annals of Human Biology,* 4, 501-23.

Tanner, J.M. (1978) *Education and Physical Growth* (2nd edition). London: Hodder and Stoughton.

Whitehead, A.N. (1955) *Aims of Education* (2nd edition). London: Benn.

Index